CW00684902

MARK WILLIAMS
YING ZHOU
MIN ZOU

MAPPING GOOD WORK

The Quality of Working Life Across the
Occupational Structure

BRISTOL
UNIVERSITY
PRESS

First published in Great Britain in 2020 by

Bristol University Press
University of Bristol
1-9 Old Park Hill
Bristol
BS2 8BB
UK
t: +44 (0)117 954 5940
e: bup-info@bristol.ac.uk

Details of international sales and distribution partners are available at bristoluniversitypress.co.uk

British Library Cataloguing in Publication Data
A catalogue record for this book is available from the British Library

ISBN 978-1-5292-0829-0 hardcover
ISBN 978-1-5292-0832-0 ePub
ISBN 978-1-5292-1609-7 OA ePDF

Cover design by Blu Inc
Front cover image: iStock / cnythzl

Bristol University Press uses environmentally responsible
print partners.

Printed in Great Britain by CPI Group (UK) Ltd,
Croydon, CR0 4YY

FSC
www.fsc.org
MIX
Paper from
responsible sources
FSC® C013604

Contents

List of Figures and Tables

Figures

Tables

List of Abbreviations

CIPD	Chartered Institute of Personnel and Development
GWI	Good Work Index
LFS	Labour Force Survey
NS-SEC	National Statistics Socio-economic Classification
OECD	Organization for Economic Co-operation and Development
OLS	ordinary least squares
ONS	Office for National Statistics
SES	Skills and Employment Survey
SOC	Standard Occupational Classification

Notes on the Authors

Mark Williams is Reader in Human Resource Management at the School of Business and Management at Queen Mary University of London, UK.

Ying Zhou is Reader in Human Resource Management at Surrey Business School at the University of Surrey, UK.

Min Zou is Associate Professor in Human Resource Management at Henley Business School at the University of Reading, UK.

Acknowledgments

Writing a book is always a challenge, but it is a fulfilling one. It certainly reminded us how having the space and freedom to make the best use of one's skills is very much central to one's own satisfaction with work. A number of people and organizations have made this book possible, or otherwise easier than it might have been. First and foremost, the support of the Economic and Social Research Council (ESRC) is gratefully acknowledged (grant numbers ES/S008470/1 and ES/S008470/2). The ESRC also contributed to much of the funding for the Skills and Employment Surveys, the main datasets used in this book. We would also like to thank Alex Bryson, Alan Felstead, Duncan Gallie, and Arne Kalleberg – all of whom commented on the grant application of which this book is the main product. Jonny Gifford at the Chartered Institute of Personnel and Development and Cara Maguire at the Department for Business, Energy and Industrial Strategy were also very supportive of the idea. At Bristol University Press (BUP), Paul Stevens, who at one very late wine reception listened to the book idea of our project before it was even funded by one of the authors, and not only remembered the conversation, but liked it enough to give us a contract. Also at BUP, Caroline Astley, who was very efficient and accommodating with all our (admittedly sometimes a bit nit-picky) requests.

There is also a wider set of acknowledgments due to a range of individuals and organizations not directly connected to the project. The team behind the Grid Enabled Occupational

Data Environment (www.geode.stir.ac.uk/index.html#Links) maintained by Paul Lambert at the University of Stirling saved us a painstaking job in labelling occupations with their freely available code. Thanks also to the UK Data Archive for hosting and documenting the data, and the survey companies conducting the surveys. Similarly, the Secure Data Service provided access to the New Earnings Panel dataset and checked and released our statistical outputs based on it, which is gratefully acknowledged.

A special thanks to the University of Surrey who granted a sabbatical to the first and second authors during which time most of the manuscript was written. At Surrey, Eugene Sadler-Smith provided encouragement for the idea of writing a book (book-writing is a surprizingly rare activity in UK business schools). Also at Surrey, Nick Jenkins was an absolute star with some IT issues which were entirely the fault of the first author. Most of all, a very special thanks to the tens of thousands of survey respondents who, over several decades, donated tens of thousands of hours all in the name of social science. We hope we have provided something interesting and useful, not just to academics and policy specialists, but to those participants as well.

Introduction

High-quality work[1] is central for a productive and thriving society. Ensuring a sufficient *quality* of work – as a policy issue – as opposed the government's conventional responsibility of ensuring a sufficient *quantity* of work – reached its zenith in the UK in July 2017 when the government published a review to scope out a new national job quality strategy. The publication, *Good Work: The Taylor Review of Modern Working Practices*, which has come to be known simply as the Taylor Review after its author Matthew Taylor, marked a turning point in UK industrial policy. It recommended the government's new 'Good Work' strategy should be more than ensuring that 'all work should be fair and decent' (that is, it pays / is stable enough to live) but that it also offers 'realistic scope for development and fulfilment'.[2] The government's response was rather positive.[3] While concern over job quality – defined more broadly than pay and security to include things like the nature of work itself – has been on the agendas of supranational organizations such as the Organization for Economic Co-operation and Development (OECD) and the European Union for years,[4] only now did the UK government authoritatively demonstrate it wanted a UK-specific national strategy on the quality of work defined in this broader sense too.[5]

In defining 'Good Work' as being work that also offers realistic scope for development and fulfilment as well as being fair and decent, the Taylor Review implicitly recognized the government should view work as a means of ensuring national well-being as well as a means to prosperity. This means that, in the UK today, the highest levels of government, at least on paper, now recognize aspects of work such as the extent to which workers have control over their work tasks and working time, the extent to which their work makes use of their skills, and their well-being from work as *central* to Good Work.[6] In this way, the Good Work agenda ties employment policy to the government's broader well-being agenda.[7]

The purpose of this book is to make visible the hierarchy in the quality of work defined in this broader sense, providing a map of how important different aspects of job quality are to workers, where higher and lower-quality jobs and occupations are more and less likely to be found, and how this has been evolving. We build on the notion that 'Good Work' is multidimensional by ultimately deferring to workers' own evaluations of what they find 'good' about work – and by how much – through correlations between different dimensions of job quality and job satisfaction. We then use these empirical insights to map out what we term the *occupational quality structure* (which can be read as the more enduring hierarchy in the quality of work given we tend to stay in the same occupation for many years) and then map out how this has been evolving. We believe that only by recognizing that some aspects of work are more important to a worker's sense of well-being than others – and mapping how the quality of work is occupationally differentiated in this regard – can we make real progress in promoting high-quality work, or Good Work, in addition to eliminating low quality or 'Bad Work'.

In mapping the contours across jobs and occupations, it is likely that aspects of job quality, although correlated with one another, do not always coincide. The best-paid occupations, for instance, might not always be the best overall when taking the broader, well-being-centred, view of what defines Good Work. Conversely, there may be some redeeming features to certain types of low-paying occupations, such as affording their incumbents a high degree of autonomy or skill-use. How job-quality dimensions trade off and how they are differentially bundled across different sorts of jobs are the critical issues we seek to explore. Moreover, as the labour market is constantly evolving, this book seeks to provide a dynamic portrait on these issues too.

In this chapter, we first briefly outline the policy context of the Good Work agenda. Next, we provide an overview the three sets of social science literature informing our mapping of Good Work in Britain. We finish by summarizing how our mapping approach can help in not only understanding the enduring disparities in the quality of work between different sections of the labour market, but also in informing practical pathways for increasing the share of workers realizing the Good Work ideal.

The Good Work agenda

Following the Taylor Review, the government is now implementing steps to improve job quality defined in the broader sense through widening the remit of the Labour Market Enforcement Agency beyond the proper enforcement of minimum standards and tasking the Office for National Statistics (ONS) with collecting and publishing national statistics on the quality of work. With respect to the latter, the Carnegie Trust set up a working group to more precisely operationalize 'Good Work' and they reported their findings in 2018.[8] Among the key recommendations made were that the government should adopt a multidimensional definition of 'Good Work'. Informed by decades of social science research, it identified the following six dimensions of job quality – with well-being being the seventh dimension – representing Good Work (with example subdimensions in brackets):

- terms of employment (job security, minimum guaranteed hours, underemployment);
- pay and benefits (pay, satisfaction with pay);
- job design and the nature of work (use of skills, control, opportunities for progression, sense of purpose);

- social support and cohesion (peer support, line manager relationship);
- voice and representation (trade union membership, employee information, employee involvement);
- work–life balance (over-employment, overtime [paid and unpaid]);
- health, safety and psychosocial well-being (job satisfaction, physical and mental health risk).

It also recommended the government map progress on these seven dimensions through the ONS's Labour Force Survey (LFS) and publish headline findings on trends in them alongside other official labour-market statistics such as the unemployment rate and wage growth, which are also often obtained from the LFS or other similar large-scale social surveys. Indicators on these dimensions are either currently being collected or are planned to be collected by the ONS (their inclusion in the LFS is staggered). The ONS published its first job quality report in November 2019.

These are huge accomplishments in promoting higher-quality work. The government now recognizes things like job design and the nature of work and well-being as a component of Good Work. However, there is a risk that the Good Work agenda gets stuck on solely eliminating low pay and insecure work, and properly enforcing labour standards,[9] or that the Good Work agenda only matters insofar as there is a business case for it[10] – as fundamental as these are. There is a risk the 'Good Work' agenda may turn into the 'Bad Work' agenda, narrowly focusing on what makes work fair and decent and sufficiently productive, with less emphasis (if any) on what makes work provide realistic scope for development, fulfilment and high job-related well-being. To make our argument as to why the Good Work agenda must *cover the full range of dimensions*, we build on three social science literatures to provide our map.

Good Work is multidimensional

Why is Good Work multidimensional anyway? Why should the government be concerned with quality of work beyond pay and security? Is not the main function of the state to keep its citizens safe and healthy? In this sense, a narrow focus on eliminating 'Bad Work' is therefore the right one. After all, what is 'good' for one worker might not be so for another, while what is 'bad' for one worker (such as having insufficient income and stability to live) *is* generally so for another. The discipline of psychology and its subfield of occupational and organizational psychology have for decades been identifying which aspects of work are more and less important for psychological well-being.[11] This stream of research has shown how intrinsic features of work – such as the extent to which it affords us the opportunities to develop and use our abilities – are fundamental to how we evaluate the quality of our work and how it makes us feel.[12] Moreover, the roles these intrinsic factors play in shaping our well-being seem largely universal, given the common human need for personal accomplishment in all life domains, including work. In other words, what is good about work may well be as universal as what is bad about work.

However, these intrinsic features of work that are known to augment job-related well-being sometimes get lost in the public and policy debates about the quality of work. The nature of what workers actually *do* in their job – the job content – and how this matters for well-being is much less discussed than how workers are fairly or unfairly compensated for it. Part of the reason might be because, while social scientists have offered very important theoretical insights, reliable data on the intrinsic dimensions of job quality are often unavailable in large-scale national surveys required to understand how critical intrinsic features of work are distributed throughout the labour market, or to establish population-level statistical regularities required for policy-making purposes. Without high-quality nationally representative data on job design and the nature of work, it is difficult to map findings based on small samples to the population level for instance, identifying which sorts of occupations have the highest well-being potential and which have the least, which occupations the government should prioritize or deprioritize for job growth, which ones are growing, which ones are declining and so on and so forth.

An occupational perspective

Much social science, particularly from the discipline of sociology and its subfield of social stratification, tells us that not all work is created equally. There are inherent inequalities in the labour market between different sorts of occupations (aggregations of functionally similar jobs) and occupational classes (aggregations of similar sorts of occupations). The differentiation in levels of pay, security and opportunities for career advancement between occupations and occupational class positions ultimately shape the 'life chances' of individuals, according to this stream of research.[13] That is, an individual's capacity to have a high quality of life depends to a large extent on their occupation, or broad field of work. Moreover, a long research tradition in economics is known as labour-market segmentation. This states that the labour market is not one large seamless market but is rather labour *markets*, which are lumpy and often divided along occupational lines.[14] This implies mobility across occupations is generally very low (we tend to stay in the same occupation for many years as career changes are an exception to the norm). For the inequalities in the quality of work, that labour markets are segmented implies that occupational inequalities endure over entire working lives.

The economic prospects of an individual in a higher managerial and professional occupation are a great order of magnitude better than someone in a routine occupation. Sociologists have established near-universal statistical regularities in this regard across countries. What is more, inequalities between class positions have become much more entrenched. In Britain today, one's occupation is a better predictor of one's lifetime earnings than it was in the 1970s and 1980s, even when unions and coordinated wage setting determined the pay for three quarters of the labour force and overall wage inequality was much lower.[15]

Nonetheless, in charting the evolution of enduring economic inequalities between different fields of work, research has focused more on pecuniary aspects of work. While statistical regularities regarding how one's occupation relates to one's economic life chances (pay and security) are well-established, we know less about how it relates to what this book terms the *quality of work life chances* defined more broadly. Knowing where the enduring positions of advantage and disadvantage are with respect to prospects for development and fulfilment at work should, therefore, be a fundamental concern. The key insights from stratification research is that the quality of work is highly stratified by the occupational structure, and sociologists have developed many tools and established population statistical-level regularities that can readily and fruitfully be applied to developing pathways for increasing the share of the labour market experiencing a high-quality work life.

For our purpose of mapping Good Work, there are three reasons for taking an occupational perspective. First, occupations provide a readily relatable unit of analysis. Not only are occupations theoretically meaningful, publishing national statistics by occupation will increase transparency in the issue for research, organizations, government and the general public – to raise awareness and benchmark about the issue. Second, occupational mobility is relatively low. We tend to stay in the same occupation for many years even if we change employer. As Figure 1.1 shows, occupational mobility accounts for only about half of all job mobility. And when we do change occupations, it tends to be one similar to the one we left. Moreover, job and occupational mobility have been declining. This all means occupations not only relate to

Figure 1.1: Trends in job and occupational mobility 1976 to 2016

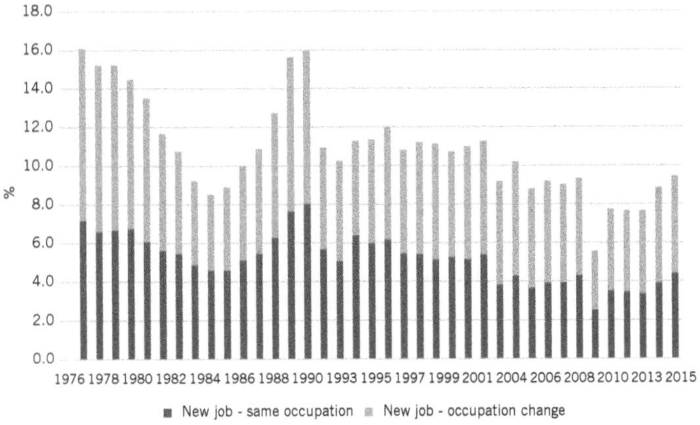

Note: All employees who appear in two or more consecutive years in the New Earnings Panel Dataset 1976 to 2016.[16]

cross-sectional disparities, but also to more enduring disparities over, potentially, entire working lives – and increasingly so. Last but not least, given occupations are often recorded based on a detailed and commonly used classification system: they can be used to impute job quality in datasets where job quality information is unavailable but occupational data exist. As we go onto show, this approach can be very useful for mapping historical and future trends in the quality of work.

The evolving structure of occupations

Much social science, in particular economics and its subfield of labour economics, tells us there have been fundamental changes in the structure of the labour market since the 1980s to 2000s, largely due to technological change. Orthodox economics approaches and traditional labour-supply models in economics paint a portrait of work as a disutility and as such has focused on pay as the central criterion for defining 'Good Work'. The key research focused on the evolution in the occupational structure in the UK distinguished between 'lovely' and 'lousy' jobs based on the average pay of the occupation and reveals that there has been a growth in both low-paying and high-paying occupations, with a huge decline in middle-paying occupations since the 1980s.[17] Studies show that much of this structural shift is due to increasing permeation and advancement of technology within workplaces, automating and replacing routine jobs (which tend to be middle-paying occupations) and complementing and expanding not only high-paying occupations, but also low-paying, non-routine ones. This narrative of a polarizing labour market with the 'hollowing out' of the middle has been – and continues to be – tremendously influential in public debates and is often (incorrectly) mapped onto debates about the quality of working life defined more broadly and the future of work.

While this stream of research has provided valuable insights into the historical and potential future trends in the labour market with respect to employees' economic rewards, we know little about how technological change and automation relate to the shifting occupational structure when occupations are ranked in terms of scope for development, fulfilment and well-being. Knowing how the labour-market structure is evolving – and how it is likely to evolve – with respect to a multidimensional definition of job quality is essential for forming effective policies to funnel the effects of technological change in more targeted ways that can have implications not just for material living standards, but national well-being. In this sense, the shifting contours in the occupational structure inform the shifting contours in the opportunity structure for Good Work.

Structure of the book

To sum up the foregoing, it is now widely recognized that Good Work is multidimensional – Good Work is not only work that is fair and decent but offers realistic scope for development and fulfilment. We seek to provide a map of Good Work in Britain, building on insights from three academic fields. In brief, organizational psychology informs us that high-quality work is necessarily more than work that pays well and is reasonably secure, and that job-related well-being provides an appropriate yardstick to understand why some aspects of work and indeed some jobs are 'more good' than others. Social stratification theory from sociology informs us that not all jobs are created equally, and that the occupational structure provides a useful way of tapping into the seemingly invisible parameters in the potential for different sections of the labour market to achieve Good Work. Economics, although tending to focus on mainly economic aspects of work, provides useful theories and tools for mapping how the structure of opportunity of Good Work is shifting, and might further evolve.

There are four central questions our book seeks to address:

1. What makes work good?
2. What is the structure of occupational quality?
3. What has been happening to the occupational quality structure since the 1980s?
4. What are the policy implications of the answers to questions 1 to 3?

Chapter One (Mapping Good Work) provides an overview of the technical aspects of mapping the quality of work. Addressing the first question, Chapter Two (What Makes Work Good?) explores what workers themselves think is good about their work – not just what academics and policy makers prescribe as good – and argues workers' own evaluations should provide an important consideration in identifying the hierarchy in the quality of work. Chapter Three (The Good Work Hierarchy) outlines an overall measure of job quality which takes into account both what matters for worker well-being and the quality of their work into a single index used in the later chapters. Addressing the second question, Chapter Four

(The Occupational Quality Structure) maps how the overall job quality metric we develop is stratified across the occupational structure. It demonstrates that the occupational quality structure is closely related to but still different from the occupational class and wage structures: there are many informative and interesting exceptions. The chapter shows that one's occupation is a fundamental determinant of how good one's job is across all job quality dimensions, and increasingly so. Addressing the third question, Chapter Five (The Changing Occupational Quality Structure) reinterprets changes in the occupational structure from a multidimensional job quality perspective, presenting a mixed picture with some grounds for genuine optimism, and some grounds for genuine pessimism. The final chapter, Chapter Six (Conclusions and Implications), addresses the final question.

ONE

Mapping Good Work

Introduction

The quality of work as a subject of study has a long history in the social sciences. This chapter is not a comprehensive review of this field of study as decent reviews exist elsewhere.[1] Rather, this chapter provides the necessary backdrop to the later chapters that map out the contours in the quality of work in Britain in detail. This chapter will first outline a very brief overview of the main social science approaches to studying the quality of work, moving on to discuss the main methods of mapping Good Work with a focus on large-scale social surveys, before closing with our main argument about the usefulness of an occupational approach for making visible disparities in the quality of work.

Approaches to the quality of work

A foundational finding in social science research is the centrality of work to the quality of life. This can be seen in studies that show a single spell of unemployment has strongly detrimental effects on individuals' physical and mental well-being lasting for many years,[2] while only eventual re-employment can erase the scars.[3] Over many decades, social scientists have also

shown that the *nature of work* is also critical and have identified a number of dimensions along which it can vary. Within
economics, orthodox economics approaches frequently treat
pay and benefits as synonymous with job quality.[4] Institutional
economics, on the other hand, has highlighted contractual
status, job stability and development opportunities offered
by the job as equally important in its dual and segmented
labour-market theories.[5] Sociological approaches, with their
intellectual roots in theories of the labour process and occupational class, have tended to emphasize security, opportunities
for advancement, skill development and control over work
processes.[6] Organizational psychologists, as mentioned in the
Introduction, have tended to emphasize more intrinsic aspects
of work. Their research frequently shows how specific aspects
of work and task organization (such as autonomy and job
demands) are important determinants of well-being and physical health.[7] Given the range of factors identified in previous
research, the newer social science field of job quality is now
an amalgamation of these disciplinary traditions and there is a
consensus that job quality is a multidimensional concept.[8] We
follow this tradition.

Building on decades of social science research and the
newer emerging field of job quality, various policy groups
have developed their own precise operationalizations of the
quality of work. Table 1.1 lists the main ones developed for the
UK context and some selected others by international policy
groups for comparison. What is striking is their similarity in
measures. They also contain all the key tenets suggested by
the three main disciplines contributing to the social science
research in this area, arriving at multidimensional definitions.
They all include an array of non-economic features of work
that are known to be central to well-being. In the next chapter,
we present some detailed analysis why these factors should be
included in policy definitions, and how important they are in
identifying the job quality hierarchy.

Table 1.1: Policy definitions

UK policy groups					International policy groups		
Taylor Review[a]	CIPD/Carnegie Trust[b]	Institute for the Future of Work[c]	Welsh Government[d]	Scottish Government[e]	Eurofound	European Trade Union Institute	OECD
Wages	Pay and benefits	Access	Fair reward	Security	Earnings	Wages	Earnings quality
Employment quality	Terms of employment	Fair pay	Employee voice and collective representation	Opportunity	Prospects	Forms of employment and job security	Labour market security
Education and training	Job design and the nature of work	Fair conditions	Security and flexibility	Fulfilment	Working time quality	Working time and work–life balance	Quality of the working environment
Working conditions	Social support and cohesion	Equality	Opportunity for access, growth and progression	Respect	Skills and discretion	Working conditions	

(continued)

Table 1.1: Policy definitions (continued)

UK policy groups					International policy groups	
Work–life balance	Health and well-being	Dignity	Safe, healthy and inclusive working environment	Effective voice	Work intensity	Skills and career development
Consultative participation and collective representation	Work–life balance	Autonomy	Legal rights respected and given substantive effect		Social environment	Collective representation
	Voice and representation	Support			Physical environment	
		Participation				
		Learning				

Notes:

a DBEIS (2017).

b CIPD (2019) and Carnegie (2018).

c IFOW (2019).

d Welsh Government (2019).

e Fair Work Convention (2016).

The Taylor Review recommended six main dimensions of job quality. This was taken forward by Carnegie Trust – who convened a national board on devising specific indicators to be included in the LFSs by the ONS for eventual publication of official statistics on the issue. The Carnegie Trust and the ONS eventually settled on the seven dimensions (six relating to job quality, with the seventh being well-being) recommended by the Chartered Institute of Personnel and Development (CIPD) based on the latter's research on the issue,[9] identifying 18 specific indicators.[10] The first ONS report on the measures available was published in November 2019.[11] The ONS plans to publish further reports as data are collected in the LFS. Given the data are not yet collected, we use existing data sources but try to stay as close to this definition as far as possible within the limits of available measures in the data. We outline how we do this in more detail next.

Surveying the quality of work

While we may have some fairly clear definition of the dimensions that constitute the quality of work or Good Work, how do we go about measuring so we can make judgements about why one job might be better than another and why? We could rate the quality of different jobs by asking expert analysts, as was traditionally done in the United States Dictionary of Occupational Titles and its replacement the Occupational Information Network (O★NET) – a large database on the tasks used in hundreds of occupations in the US.[12] This is based on thousands of observation studies involving armies of independent analysists evaluating jobs directly through observations as they are being performed. It is, of course, hugely expensive. The latest iterations of O★NET now also ask workers to directly rate the different tasks in their jobs to economize on costs. There is the additional issue arising from the act of workers being observed influencing the data collection.[13] In most cases, workers are likely to know more about their job than their supervisor, human resources managers or external experts. This is especially true when it comes to the intrinsic aspects of work.

Typically, then, social scientists find out about people's jobs through survey questionnaires filled out by the workers themselves. Psychologists have paved the way not only in theories connecting factors that matter for well-being, but in making visible the previously thought unmeasurable – not just in terms of psychological well-being but in terms of more intrinsic aspects of work such as the amount of control we have over our tasks, or their variety – through the development of an array of validated scales.[14] Typically survey items and scales have gone through rigorous statistical testing, or validation. Indicators must be shown to be reliable and valid measures of what they are supposed to measuring.

With some notable exceptions, psychologists have traditionally not attempted to make their results representative of and therefore generalizable to any specific population. This is in direct contrast to early psychometrics and social statistics (and indeed the whole frequentist statistical paradigm) that was based on the identification of statistical regularities that can be generalized to a whole population. Sociologists, on the other hand, have championed the use of the social survey as the mainstay for identifying and explaining statistical regularities. Some even go as far to argue sociology is a 'population science'.[15] The social survey is a stalwart method of describing social reality in sociology and the population sciences more generally (including demography, epidemiology and social statistics). Social surveys are nationally representative samples. They also tend to be very high quality as data from hundreds of questions in interviews lasting typically more than an hour are collected face-to-face at the respondent's home – with sample sizes ranging from several thousands to hundreds of thousands. This also means they are probably one of the most expensive research methods in any social science. For instance, the latest Skills and Employment Survey – the main data source for this book and the richest survey on aspects of job quality – cost in the region of £1 million.[16]

In the UK context, we are very fortunate. There are a variety of representative datasets with detailed information on the quality of work therein, to varying degrees. Table 1.2 summarizes the main data sources along with their strengths and weaknesses. More thorough reviews exist elsewhere.[17]

Social surveys are not without issue, however, even in the UK context. Each dataset has advantages and disadvantages. One big disadvantage is no representative dataset including a full range of job quality indicators exists. We use the Skills and Employment Survey (SES) because it has the greatest breadth in indicators and has been running since 1986, allowing us to map over time trends.[18] However, even though it is nationally representative of England, Scotland and Wales (not consistently covering Northern Ireland or outer Scotland), the sample sizes mean we have to make some compromises along the way – especially when we examine the quality of work at the level of detailed occupational categories. For instance, we have to merge about 100 of the 353 occupational categories to give sufficient sample sizes within them. At the time of writing, a total of 18 items are to be included in the LFS.[19] Until all of those data are collected, the SES remains one of the best surveys of its kind in the world, even if our goal is to produce quite fine-grained estimates, for instance at the detailed occupational level.

Making visible disparities in the quality of work

A crucial element of our mapping approach concerns the utility of occupations in making the issue of the quality of work visible, particularly in terms of enduring disparities across not just jobs but entire careers. Why might occupations be a good unit of analysis for this? Social stratification theory in sociology puts occupation as the backbone to the stratification in life chances. In various ways and for various reasons, occupations are the unit

Table 1.2: Social surveys measuring job quality

Survey name	Years covered	Key strengths	Key weaknesses
Skills and Employment Surveys (SES)	1986, 1992, 1997, 2001, 2012, 2012, 2017	• Very rich on job quality indicators • Nationally representative • Long-running survey	• Fairly small sample sizes
Understanding Society Surveys (USS)	Annually 2010 to 2017	• Panel survey • Large sample sizes	• More limited job quality indicators
British Household Panel Surveys (BHPS)	Annually 1991 to 2008	• Panel survey • Long-running survey • Sample incorporated into USS	• Very limited job quality indicators
Labour Force Surveys (LFS)	Annually 1973 to 1991; quarterly 1992 to present	• Long-running • Very large sample sizes	• Very limited job quality indicators
Workplace Employment Relations Surveys (WERS)	1998, 2004, 2011 (there were also earlier workplace-only surveys that did not sample employees; WERS has been discontinued but some continuity will be possible with the Management and Wellbeing Practices Survey which began in 2019)	• Workplace information • Good job quality information	• Employees only

(continued)

Table 1.2: Social surveys measuring job quality (continued)

Survey name	Years covered	Key strengths	Key weaknesses
UK Working Lives Survey (UKWLS)	2018, 2019, 2020	• Very rich on job quality indicators • Contains data on meaningfulness • Panel element	• Not nationally representative – quota sample

analysis of choice for denoting the contours of advantage and disadvantage. Occupations are groups of functionally similar jobs. For example, GPs and cardiologists are different sorts of jobs on one level in that a GP could not hope to apply for a cardiology job and vice versa. However, both share a broadly similar job function of applying medical knowledge to improve the health of patients. Therefore, both belong to the broader occupation of medical practitioners. Their job roles are similar enough in their skills requirements and job content, and so pay, security and job quality, that they can be aggregated into a distinct group. Occupational classifications systems typically delineate hundreds of occupations in this way. The input information from social surveys are the respondent's job title and a written description of their job content and duties. Using a series of structured rules and algorithms overseen by a trained coder, this information is used to allocate the respondent to one of hundreds of occupation categories from directors and chief executives and senior officials, to secondary education teaching professionals, to records clerks and assistants, to shelf fillers. In the UK, the main classification is called the Standard Occupational Classification (SOC) and is devised by the ONS.

Sociologists and social statisticians have long been interested in occupations because they proxy for many socio-economic phenomena we cannot readily measure without additional survey space. It is for this reason that questions on occupation were first added to the UK Census in 1831 and have been recorded ever since. Sociologists often aggregate these detailed occupation codes into even broader groups, known as occupational classes (for example, higher managerial and professional, lower managerial and professional, and so on). There are various ways to aggregate occupations to classes depending on what one wants to use respondents' occupation to theoretically represent. Marxian approaches (following in the footsteps of Karl Marx) tend to privilege the distinction between capital (business owners), agents of capital (managers and supervisors) and labour (workers) in defining the class hierarchy. Approaches in the Weberian tradition (following in the footsteps of Max Weber) posit that there is a hierarchy within the broad class of labour, based on skills. An influential model for allocating occupations to classes in the Weberian tradition is that associated with John Goldthorpe of Nuffield College, Oxford and colleagues, which classifies occupations on employment relations. Employment relations in turn lead to life chances. For instance, accountants' employment is regulated in a broadly similar way to medical practitioners, and so both share similar levels of income and security. Both in turn are classified with higher managerial and professional occupations. Bakers' and electricians' employments are regulated in a far different way from the former two occupations but are far like each other, and so belong to the class of lower supervisory and technical occupations. From this, we can then begin to identify a hierarchy in occupations in terms of their employment relations. These positions in turn are said to be what determines differential life chances in society. In short, sociologists have shown we can say a lot about a respondent with just the tiny bits of original input information about their job title and key duties.

Occupational class – denoting broad positions of advantage and disadvantage based on relations at work and with the labour market – has a rich history in the British context. A key area of research were social mobility studies (the tendency of offspring to occupy similar socio-economic positions (occupations) to their parents). Social mobility rates are considered an important indicator of the openness and the extent of meritocracy in a society. Given the aim of this research tradition of making generalizations to whole populations, the key methodological tool to know social mobility rates for a society – something not readily visible from the perspective of an individual – is through social survey (large sample surveys that are representative of the population). Sociologists working on these and related topics pioneered the methodology, with social mobility studies playing a central role. Social surveys are now routinely used throughout the world to make transparent population-level trends like unemployment rates, levels of inflation, health and so on.

It should be noted that other stratification research defines an occupational hierarchy of social stratification in different ways and not just in terms of class, for instance, as work that enjoys high amounts of prestige or social status. Researchers have developed prestige scales and indicators quantify these. At the root of all social stratification approaches to defining social hierarchies (whether class, prestige or status) are occupations. In practice, different constructs for measuring social stratification by occupation are usually highly correlated.[20]

So back to the original question, why occupations? One answer is that occupation represents a key indicator of one's socio-economic status and the majority of people do not change occupations very often. In this way, one's occupation is considered an important determinant of one's life chances. A more pragmatic reason for our focus on occupations is that we cannot possibly measure all the complex things that relate to social stratification in every survey – and all the items and survey space. Information on occupation is a core ingredient of most social surveys, so this information can be usefully extended to proxy for specific social hierarchies such as class, prestige and status by imputing scores from other surveys based on occupation.

Class schemas, however, are not strictly intended to capture disparities in the quality of work, but rather other social hierarchies of interest. To what extent can your occupational class tell you how satisfying your line of work will be? Take the example of accountants and bakers. While they have stark differences in pay, is being an accountant necessarily better than being a baker, all things considered? At present, we do not know the answers to such questions. We contend the answers will be highly useful to promoting the Good Work agenda. Occupations are a readily relatable unit of analysis, while many of the dimensions of Good Work may appear quite abstract to the uninitiated.

Given the central importance of occupation for shaping individuals' life chances, we believe it provides an appropriate basis for mapping more enduring disparities in the quality of work defined more broadly than economic life chances. The tools developed by sociologists to map other social hierarchies can be extended to what we term the quality of work life chances, defined multidimensionally to incorporate the more intrinsic features of work highlighted by psychologists and sociologists. In other words, our goal is to develop an indicator of occupational quality that is based on multiple dimensions of job quality for the specific purpose of knowing more about the overall quality of a job where more specific job quality items have not been measured. While relying on occupational proxies might be seen as a weakness, given mobility across occupations is very low, occupational quality, then, denotes the capacity or chances of a particular line of work to lead to high job-related well-being.

To index or not to index?

While the current attitude to the measurement and mapping of policy approaches to the quality of work argues that they should be multidimensional (that is, based on multiple indicators covering different dimensions of job quality), it does not preclude the development of summary measures that put all the information together into an index. Indexes are useful for making transparent hierarchies and are widely used for this purpose. There are two main types: cross-national and job level. Regarding the former, the European Trade Union Institute using the European Working Conditions Survey and the European LFS came up with a metric to rank countries according to cross-national differences in the quality of work based on multiple dimensions. They come up with a scoring system that ranges from 0 to 100 for each dimension. These are then standardized and averaged to come up with a single score. A disadvantage of this approach, however, is that each dimension is weighted equally, meaning resultant scores are based on a metric that lacks any substantive meaning. The second way attempts to put an overall job quality score for individual jobs and not countries. However, these suffer from the same problem in that the constituent components are weighted equally or are differentially weighted arbitrarily by the analyst.[21] A single metric is especially useful when the goal is to explore stratification across many groups – as is our goal in mapping the job and occupational quality structures. We discuss a simple solution to the weighting issue based on the extent to which each dimension of job quality matters to workers.

Others argue for a 'dashboard' approach: considering the multiple dimensions separately and qualitatively constructing narratives across them.[22] The SES team advocates this approach[23] as did the Carnegie's Measuring Job Quality Working Group.[24] The CIPD follow something of a compromise in generating a set of indices, with each one representing a dimension of job quality, but the dimensions are not combined into an overall index.[25] The ONS, in their first publication on job quality, which was on the quality of working time, adopted a threshold approach based on a composite index of several indicators on this single dimension of job quality.[26]

The advantage of analysing job quality dimensions separately is that it provides a more nuanced picture. This is especially useful if the goal is to explore changes over time, as different dimensions may move in different directions, which may be obscured if they were combined into a single overall job quality metric. Given our main goal is to explore stratification across jobs and occupations, it is helpful to have a single index to define an overall hierarchy along a substantively meaningful metric. We contend that it may still be useful to have an overall job quality index even if one's goal is to map over time changes. It just needs to be theoretically and empirically sound, such that the numbers are ultimately substantively meaningful. We outline our approach in Chapter Three. Clearly, the solution to the debate about whether to index or not is to follow both approaches – it ultimately depends on the research goal.

Before closing this chapter, we elaborate further on a point made earlier about stratification. As theories of social stratification in sociology, based on the Weberian notion of life chances, an approach to mapping the quality of work should ultimately be about the *potential* that a job can be good for its incumbent rather than how good its incumbent personally finds it. That is, the *quality of work life chances*. Making visible this structure is the goal for mapping the job quality and the occupational quality structures. Thus it is helpful to develop a metric that speaks to this important theoretical point.

Summary and conclusions

• Social sciences have long studied the quality of work, and only more recently have the approaches been synthesized into an interdisciplinary field – which is proving very influential to policy. Building on the pioneering work by social scientists that demonstrated a good job is more than one that pays well and is reasonably secure, these policy definitions typically focus on several dimensions of job quality, including intrinsic features of work that are known to be critical for job-related well-being.

- In order to know the quality of work, the nationally representative social survey method of asking workers directly to
aggregate responses and identify population-level statistical
regularities has been used to great effect. The UK has many
high-quality datasets in this regard and the government is
taking steps to improve them even further by including
multiple indicators of job quality in the LFS as part of their
Good Work agenda.
- We identified the insights from stratification theory –
which purports that not all work is created equally – and
that one's occupation shapes one's 'life chances' – as being
a very useful insight to mapping Good Work. We extend
this notion that one's occupation might shape the 'quality
of work life chances'.
- Given our interest in mapping stratification in the quality
of work, especially across occupational positions, we need
to create an index to rank jobs and occupations. An index
might also be useful for mapping general national progress,
but we see the main advantage as defining a hierarchy to
explore the structure of stratification in the quality of work
defined more broadly than pay and security.

TWO

What Makes Work Good?

Introduction

Social science and policy approaches recognize how the quality of work is multidimensional, more than just pay and security, putting well-being central, and including certain intrinsic features of work related to the work itself such as job design and the nature of work. We aim to integrate this approach with a stratification perspective, emphasizing the unequal nature of the quality of work. In identifying the quality of work hierarchy, to be sure, it is necessary to ask workers themselves what they think is good about their work. We also need to know *by how much* each different dimension makes work good, as there are reasons to believe different dimensions are not equally important, in their evaluations. This chapter explores various ways of knowing this, including looking at the correlation between job quality dimensions and job satisfaction. While job satisfaction, as this chapter outlines, is inadequate on its own for indicating clearly the position of a job in the overall hierarchy, job satisfaction can still convey useful information about what makes one job better than another and by how much.

The views of workers

To better understand how multiple dimensions that comprise the quality of work should be combined to make an overall index, we ultimately need to hear from workers themselves. Furthermore, we also need to see how universal these evaluations are across different personal and work situations to see whether it is fair to assume what is 'good' for one worker is also 'good' for another. How do we do this? There are three main ways to identify what workers think is good about work and by how much: one direct way and two indirect ones. The direct way is by simply asking workers. The SES asked respondents to rate the importance 15 different aspects of work on scale of 1 ('Not very important') to 4 ('Essential'). The exact question wording is in Table 2.1. We can surmise that those dimensions that score more highly on the scale are those that workers desire most.

The second way, the first of the indirect ways, uses reported satisfaction with specific aspects of work to predict overall job satisfaction. The SES asked respondents to rate how satisfied they were with 14 different aspects of work and another item asking them to sum up their job satisfaction overall, all rated on a scale from 1 (completely dissatisfied) to 7 (completely satisfied).[1] The full question wording is given in Table 2.2. Using a simple ordinary least squares (OLS) regression, we can determine the relative influence of satisfaction with these different facets in influencing their overall job satisfaction.[2] A larger coefficient on a particular job satisfaction domain implies that this aspect weighs more heavily in respondent's overall evaluation of their job, implying this factor should contribute more to an overall job quality index.

The third way, and the second indirect way, asks workers to report objective information about different dimensions of their job and then correlates these with their overall job satisfaction. This is different from the preceding indirect way which correlates respondents' *subjective appraisals* of different facets of their job with overall job satisfaction. More concretely, take pay

Table 2.1: Work orientations survey question in the SES

I am going to read out a list of some of the things people may look for in a job and I would like you to tell me how important you feel each is for you, choosing your answer from the card:
- Good promotion prospects
- Good pay
- Good relations with your supervisor or manager
- A secure job
- A job where you can use your initiative
- Work you like doing
- Convenient hours of work
- Choice in your hours of work
- The opportunity to use your abilities
- Good fringe benefits
- An easy workload
- Good training provision
- Good physical working conditions
- A lot of variety in the type of work
- Friendly people to work with

Possible answers:
1. Not very important
2. Fairly important
3. Very important
4. Essential

for instance. While the preceding way correlates *satisfaction* with pay with overall job satisfaction to ascertain how important a role pay plays in deciding overall job satisfaction, this third way correlates *actual* rates of pay with overall job satisfaction. It is important to do both exercises as they might not give the same answer. Feelings about pay might more strongly affect overall job satisfaction than actual rates of pay for example. This is because subjective appraisals about facets of work are affected by many other things as well as the actual underlying conditions of work, such as expectations and cognitive biases. These sorts of issues – and why job satisfaction is not a suitable index on its own for mapping the quality of work – are returned to later in the chapter.

Table 2.2: Job satisfaction survey question in the SES

Overall, how satisfied are you with...
- Your promotion prospects
- Your pay
- Relations with your supervisor or manager
- Your job security
- The opportunity to use your abilities
- Being able to use your own initiative
- The ability and efficiency of the management
- The hours you work
- Fringe benefits
- The work itself
- The amount of work
- The variety in the work
- The training provided
- The friendliness of the people you work with
- All in all, how satisfied are you with your job?

Possible answers:
1. Completely dissatisfied
2. Very dissatisfied
3. Fairly dissatisfied
4. Very satisfied
5. Neither satisfied nor dissatisfied
6. Fairly satisfied
7. Completely satisfied

To summarize thus far, we have three different ways to assess the extent to which different dimensions of job quality matter to workers: (1) simply ask them; (2) observe correlations between subject appraisals of different dimensions of work with subjective appraisals of their job overall; and (3) observe correlations in how their job objectively scores on various aspects of work with subjective appraisals of their job overall. Each way has their own advantages and disadvantages. Before reporting the results of these, it is worth noting how to deal with potential variation in the weights placed on different job qualities by workers. To be sure, therefore, we must also break down the results by meaningful groups to check the universality assumption. As well as reporting overall results to these three exercises, the following analysis therefore also presents the results broken down by year, occupational class, hours of work, age, gender and ethnicity.

Turning to the results of the first way (simply asking workers), Figure 2.1 reports averages in importance respondents say they place on the different aspects when looking for a job. To get a very general picture of enduring work orientations this pools some 20,000 survey responses together from all SES waves where these items appeared stretching back 25 years (specifically the years 1992, 2006, 2012 and 2017 – the survey years in which these questions were asked). Surprisingly, perhaps,

Figure 2.1: Average importance of various aspects of work

Unstandardized coefficients

Notes: All workers aged 20 to 60 in the Skills and Employment Surveys 1992, 2006, 2012 and 2017. Data are weighted. Model includes controls for survey year, gender, age, whether non-white ethnic group, whether have children, 11 UK regions, holding a degree-level qualification, whether part-time or full-time, whether self-employed or an employee, whether on a temporary or permanent contract, whether their workplace is unionized, three workplace size dummies, four industrial sector indicators, and occupational class dummies. Horizontal lines are 95% confidence intervals.

given the conventional economists' view of what most matters to workers, pay is only in the middle, ranking the seventh most important factor overall. Those factors ranking below pay might be considered other extrinsic factors of work, such as number of hours and fringe benefits. Having an easy workload, perhaps also surprisingly given the standard assumptions about human nature in standard labour-supply models in economics, ranks last by some margin. Apart from job security, which ranks second, all the factors that rank above pay might be considered more intrinsic aspects of work, with finding work itself enjoyable the most important factor overall. Thus, the model of work being a trade-off effort for compensation appears to provide a very misleading picture of what matters to workers. Quite clearly, the content and nature of work is also – if not more – critical, as theories from psychology would predict. Therefore, these sorts of factors should weigh more heavily in constructing an overall job quality index. Controlling for other confounding factors[3] does not change the general pattern.

Now one might question whether these rankings of the importance of different aspects of work might vary according to personal and work situation. Not all workers may be alike. Figure 2.2 breaks down the results by group. The first panel is by survey year. While there is some change over the years, for example there was a slight growth in the average rating for promotion prospects (perhaps reflecting diminishing promotion prospects for many), there is remarkable stability in the overall patterns year-to-year.[4] Similarly, when we break down the averages by occupational class, hours of work, age, gender and ethnicity, we find that having enjoyable work and good job security are considered as important than pay, if not more so. The two main conclusions we can draw from this exercise for any definition of overall job quality are, first, that intrinsic factors of work clearly matter to workers when you ask them directly and thus should be given greater weight. And second, that these general patterns are similar across groups so we can tentatively assume what is Good Work for one worker is also

Figure 2.2: Average importance of various aspects of work by group

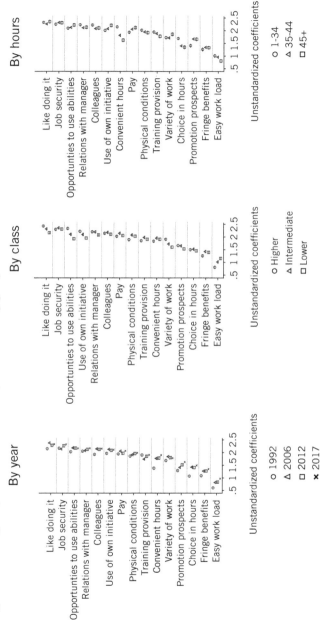

(Continued)

Figure 2.2: Average importance of various aspects of work by group (continued)

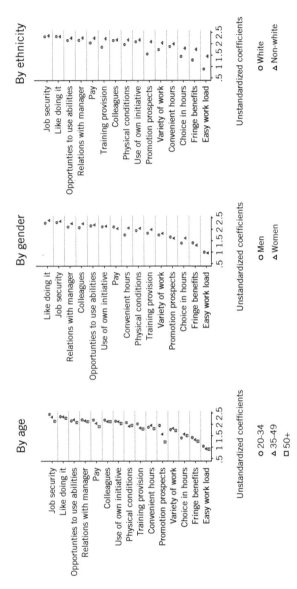

Notes: All workers aged 20 to 60 in the Skills and Employment Surveys 1992, 2006, 2012 and 2017. Data are weighted. Model includes controls for survey year, gender, age, whether non-white ethnic group, whether have children, 11 UK regions, holding a degree-level qualification, whether part-time or full-time, whether self-employed or an employee, whether on a temporary or permanent contract, whether their workplace is unionized, three workplace size dummies, four industrial sector indicators, and occupational class dummies. Horizontal lines are 95% confidence intervals.

Good Work for another, providing face validity to constructing a hierarchical index.

One may object that what people say matters to them might be different from what *actually* matters to them.[5] There are many reasons why stated preferences might vary from actual or latent preferences, social desirability being one (the survey data ultimately comes from face-to-face interviews), but also other cognitive biases. Hence, we turn to two indirect ways to identify what workers believe to be Good Work. The first of these uses worker ratings about their satisfaction with various aspects of work to predict their ratings of overall job satisfaction. This in effect quantifies the unconscious relative contributions of satisfaction with different aspects of work made by respondents in arriving at their overall job satisfaction assessment. In Figure 2.3, we find that intrinsic factors of work matter a great deal. By far the strongest predictor of overall job satisfaction is satisfaction with the work itself. Workers who are satisfied with the work itself, tend to be the most satisfied overall by quite a margin. By contrast, being very satisfied with fringe benefits, for instance, makes very little difference to overall job satisfaction, implying that, when workers are making global judgements about their job, these barely enter the decision-making process. This highlights that the Taylor Review's call for placing development and fulfilment central to the definition of Good Work is very much supported by workers themselves.

One of the advantages of multivariable analysis is that we can hold constant (control for) confounding factors. When we introduce control variables, the picture remains unchanged. Interestingly, even when we additionally control for the importance ratings workers attach to different aspects of work used in Figure 2.1 and Figure 2.2, the picture still remains the same. That is, even controlling for possible heterogeneity in what workers say they value, the overall patterns do not change. Interestingly, and as a side point, what these results imply is that much of the vast literature on overall job satisfaction can then be read as largely about satisfaction with the work itself.

Turning to how these predictive relationships vary according to group (Figure 2.4), again, we find remarkable consistency to the overall picture: satisfaction with the work itself is the most important factor for overall satisfaction, implying a near-universal pattern that intrinsic features of work matter most.

However, there are *some* discrepancies between what workers report as mattering to them (the preceding exercise) and what

Figure 2.3: Predictive effects of satisfaction with various aspects of work on overall job satisfaction

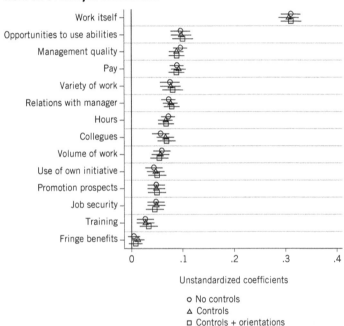

Unstandardized coefficients

o No controls
△ Controls
□ Controls + orientations

Notes: All workers aged 20 to 60 in the Skills and Employment Surveys 2006, 2012 and 2017. Data are weighted. Model includes controls for survey year, gender, age, whether non-white ethnic group, whether have children, 11 UK regions, holding a degree-level qualification, whether part-time or full-time, whether self-employed or an employee, whether on a temporary or permanent contract, whether their workplace is unionized, three workplace size dummies, four industrial sector indicators, and occupational class dummies. Horizontal lines are 95% confidence intervals.

Figure 2.4: Predictive effects of satisfaction with various aspects of work on overall job satisfaction by group

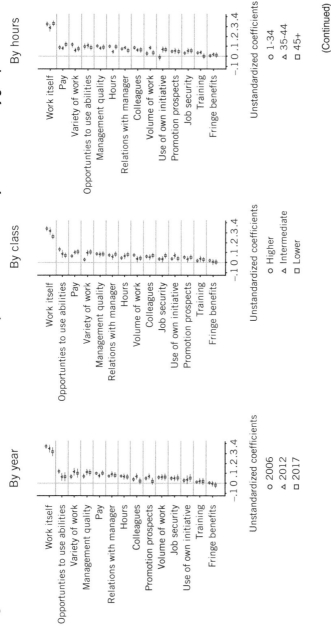

(Continued)

Figure 2.4: Predictive effects of satisfaction with various aspects of work on overall job satisfaction by group (continued)

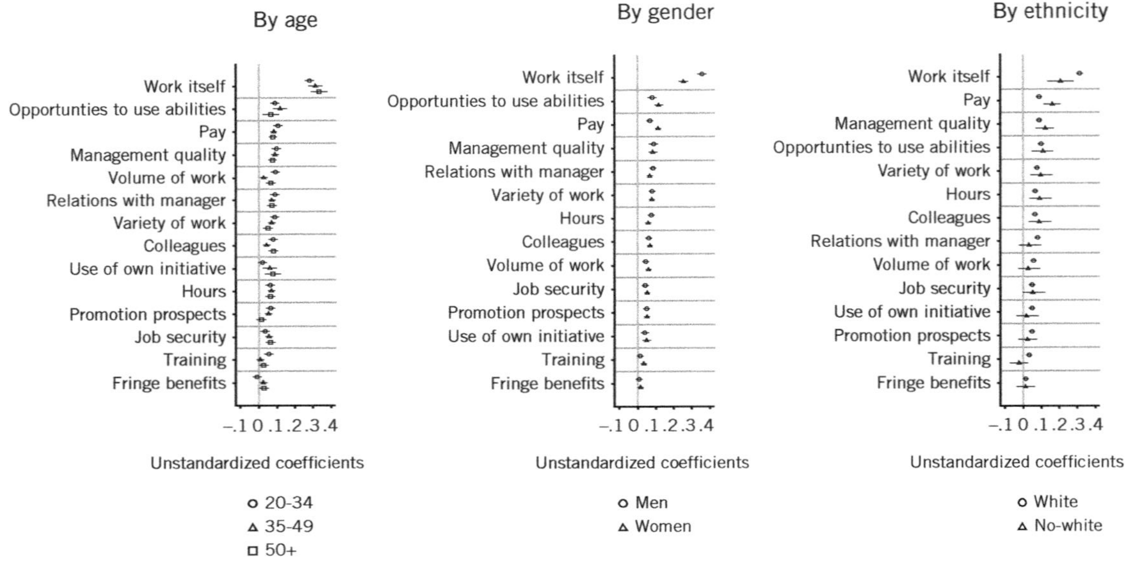

Notes: All workers aged 20 to 60 in the Skills and Employment Surveys 2006, 2012 and 2017. Data are weighted. Model includes controls for survey year, gender, age, whether non-white ethnic group, whether have children, 11 UK regions, holding a degree-level qualification, whether part-time or full-time, whether self-employed or an employee, whether on a temporary or permanent contract, whether their workplace is unionized, three workplace size dummies, four industrial sector indicators, and occupational class dummies. Horizontal lines are 95% confidence intervals.

influences their overall satisfaction judgements about their jobs (this exercise). For instance, workers rate job security highly when asked about what they look for in a job but when making assessments about their overall satisfaction, satisfaction with job security seems to factor only in a smaller way in that decision. Again, this could reflect cognitive biases, so it is important to triangulate the findings from a set of exercises rather than just one.

Next, we turn to the third exercise, the second indirect way: exploring the relationship between observed job quality and overall job satisfaction. This third exercise correlates objective features of work with overall job satisfaction to ascertain how important each is when workers are deciding how good their job is through their overall job satisfaction ratings. More information on how these job qualities are measured can be found in the next chapter. Since all the facets of job quality in Table 3.1 are measured on different scales, they are standardized here to have a mean of 0 and a standard deviation of 1 (z-scores). The common scale is therefore in standard deviations. The results are reported in Figure 2.5. Skill-use opportunities stand as the most important factor for overall job satisfaction. Next important are task variety and job security, with task discretion not far behind. Introducing controls,[6] as well as including measures of how important different aspects of work are to respondents used in Figure 2.1, makes little difference to these findings. Perhaps surprisingly, pay and job demands appear to have small effects that are indistinguishable from zero once all factors are controlled.[7] On the other hand, as the earlier analysis revealed, aspects related to the work itself more strongly relate to overall job satisfaction than more extrinsic factors. Nonetheless, job security comes out as very important. That is why any hierarchy should not be solely about intrinsic features of work – but should be multidimensional.

When exploring these patterns by group, as with the previous analyses, little changes in terms of the overall story

Figure 2.5: Predictive effects of job quality (standardized) on overall job satisfaction

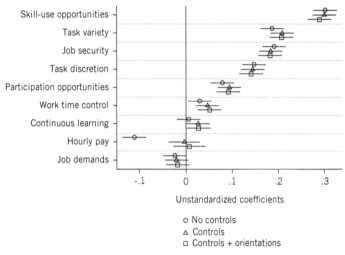

Notes: All workers aged 20 to 60 in the Skills and Employment Surveys 2006, 2012 and 2017. Data are weighted. Model includes controls for survey year, gender, age, whether non-white ethnic group, whether have children, 11 UK regions, holding a degree-level qualification, whether part-time or full-time, whether self-employed or an employee, whether on a temporary or permanent contract, whether their workplace is unionized, three workplace size dummies, four industrial sector indicators, and occupational class dummies. Horizontal lines are 95% confidence intervals.

(see Figure 2.6). Once again, these findings demonstrate that intrinsic aspects of work are critical to distinguishing what is good about work, even across different sorts of workers and work situations.

The overall conclusion from these exercises is that intrinsic features of work matter dearly to workers when they are deciding how to rate how good their job is. Clearly, then, any metric of Good Work must not only include them but give them their due weight when combined into an index. The other secondary conclusion is that these general patterns do not vary a great deal across different types of

Figure 2.6: Predictive effects of job quality on overall job satisfaction by group

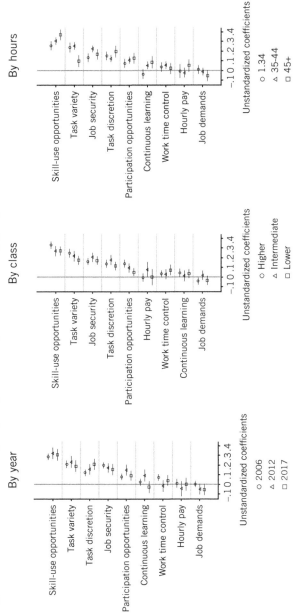

(Continued)

Figure 2.6: Predictive effects of job quality on overall job satisfaction by group (continued)

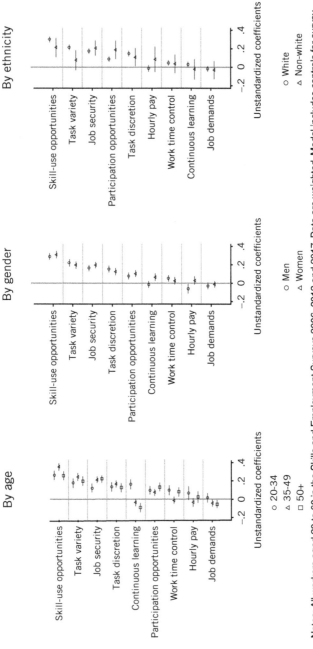

Notes: All workers aged 20 to 60 in the Skills and Employment Surveys 2006, 2012 and 2017. Data are weighted. Model includes controls for survey year, gender, age, whether non-white ethnic group, whether have children, 11 UK regions, holding a degree-level qualification, whether part-time or full-time, whether self-employed or an employee, whether on a temporary or permanent contract, whether their workplace is unionized, three workplace size dummies, four industrial sector indicators, and occupational class dummies. Horizontal lines are 95% confidence intervals.

workers. What is good for one worker is, broadly speaking, good for another.

Job satisfaction ≠ job quality

Before describing how these exercises can inform the weighting in constructing the Good Work Index (GWI), it is helpful to first give more of a rationale about why we need to go to the trouble of developing an index in the first place and not simply rely on reports of overall job satisfaction themselves as an overall metric. It is tempting, of course. If workers know their job better than anyone else and it is up to them ultimately to decide to what extent they find their job fulfilling, why not just use overall job satisfaction to define the overall hierarchy in the quality of work? For instance, in order to understand how the quality of work is stratified, we could simply rank jobs and occupations by overall job satisfaction. Or to explore trends in overall quality of work over time, we could simply track what has been happening to job satisfaction.

There are some pros to this sort of argument. One advantage is that relying solely on job satisfaction would capture *everything* about the job – not just its pay, security, learning, task variety and so on – but all other things that can be said to make one job better than another, such as things like the social status attached to it, how well the job matches idiosyncratic preferences and expectations, and so on. However, there are some cons. While self-reported job satisfaction is an incredibly useful metric – and one we know a great deal about – it cannot be, and is not, an indicator of quality of a job in and of itself. While job satisfaction (and other attitudinal and affective well-being measures) are critical to validating the factors we think might underlie the quality of work and telling us how important they are to the overall quality of a particular job, job satisfaction itself is not an objective feature of the job. Job satisfaction – like life satisfaction – is affected by:

- Expectations: job satisfaction is affected by people's expectations and how those expectations match up to reality. It is affected by people's personal biases and preferences. For instance, there is an enduring tendency for women to have higher job satisfaction than men. It would be inaccurate to conclude from this that women tend to occupy better jobs than men. Job satisfaction partly measures what psychologists called person–job fit.

- Adaptation: in the psychology literature there is a well-known process labelled the honeymoon-hangover effect regarding job changes whereby job satisfaction increases sharply when starting a new job, but that quickly falls back to the original level.[8] Similar findings are found in the life satisfaction literature with respect to life events.[9] People ultimately return to baseline. Or to put it another way, they adapt to the situation. A well-known paradox in the life satisfaction research is the Easterlin paradox (named after the researcher who popularized it). Easterlin found that although richer countries are on average happier than poorer ones, as countries became richer, they did not get any happier.

- Social comparisons: another insight from the research into job and life satisfaction is that relative position in various hierarchies matter. Research has shown that absolute levels of income are not what necessarily matter most to well-being, but relative levels are equally (if not more) important – how much one earns relative to a relevant reference.[10] When we think about how satisfied we are with our own pay, we do not (unfortunately) think how well we are doing in the entire distribution of pay, only relative to those doing similar jobs to us (like our colleagues or those in the same occupation).[11]

- Personality: though the effect of personality on job satisfaction is much weaker than it is for life satisfaction,[12] neurotics report lower job satisfaction, while extroverts report higher job satisfaction on average.[13]

What this sort of research implies for mapping job quality is that if underlying (and objective) job quality increased, job satisfaction would not necessarily increase because workers quickly get used to it (adaptation).[14] Similarly, if we could measure all possible dimensions of job quality and found they all substantially increased but relative differences in them remained constant, there might be no change in job satisfaction (social comparisons). Although everyone is better off, everyone is better off equally. Finally, they suggest that different individuals might find different aspects of work fulfilling due to their realistic labour-market prospects and personal quirks (expectations and personality). Modelling this at the aggregate level is not very helpful for policy because it is dynamic and very idiosyncratic. It only partly conveys information about the quality of the job, as well as conveying the personal quirks and non-work situations of the individual filling out the survey. Rather, what is needed is a more standardized approach that works for the general working population, more of a one-size-fits-all approach, that is comparable across individuals, irrespective of their personal quirks.

Overall reports of job satisfaction, though, are a useful tool to help us understand how important different aspects of job quality are for workers – which helps in meaningfully combining multiple dimensions in constructing overall indices. This is in turn better than using work orientations as weights because what workers say they want and what would benefit their satisfaction are not necessarily one and the same (as the finding about job security showed). Additionally, overall job satisfaction – being a single measure – makes any weighting procedure simpler than having multiple measures and multiple weights.

In sum, the overall hierarchy in the quality of work is not synonymous with the overall hierarchy in job satisfaction, but rather the *potential of a job to be satisfying for the average worker based on a common basket of job qualities*. The GWI, which we outline in detail in the next chapter, provides an illustration of a method to obtain a hierarchy in multiple job quality dimensions across jobs. Although individual's quirks, of course, matter to a certain extent, as the aforementioned exercises demonstrate, there is a striking resemblance between what workers say are important to them and which job quality factors have the strongest effect on ratings of overall job satisfaction. Of the measures in the SES, by far the three most important are skill-use, task variety and job security. Perhaps surprisingly to some readers, pay and job demands appear to have a much smaller influence. These findings highlight that high-quality work is not simply about having higher levels of job satisfaction, but having higher amounts of those things that are generally important to job satisfaction. This is not to say that if one has all these things one would be very satisfied, given, as mentioned, that job satisfaction is influenced by many other things in addition to a core set of job qualities. This may be of little practical use for individuals given few 'average' people exist, but to a government interested in a national or population-level picture, it is of great use. While our main goal in developing this way of viewing job quality is to identify the overall hierarchy in the quality of jobs and occupations, the perspective might be useful for mapping trends in the quality of work over time and place.

Summary and conclusions

- This chapter reviewed what is good about work in order to illustrate why the quality of work is necessarily about more than pay and security. It argued the best way to know what is good about work – and how good – is to ask workers themselves. It presented various ways this can be done. It generally found the nature of work – the job content – to be the most important, though job security is up there. It supports the notion that Good Work is work that is fair and decent but also has realistic scope for development and fulfilment.

- In particular skill-use, task variety and task discretion were found to be most important. Job security was also found to be very important, while pay and job demands were found to be of middling importance. These findings are useful in informing us how to combine different job qualities together in mapping the overall hierarchy in the quality of work, as there is a hierarchy in the different dimensions of job quality themselves.
- It also outlined that job satisfaction is an important metric for understanding how we can rank the importance of different job qualities for workers, but job satisfaction itself cannot be used as an indicator of job quality since it contains information that is extraneous to the job, such as individual quirks relating to expectations, personal situations, social comparisons and personality.

THREE

The Good Work Hierarchy

Introduction

Although analysing many dimensions separately provides a more nuanced picture of the quality of work (the 'dashboard approach'), it is helpful to have some way of ranking jobs and occupations for our purposes of mapping its stratified nature, its hierarchy. To be able to say one job (or indeed one occupation) is better than another or whether the quality of work is generally improving or not – and by how much – we need to be able to score all jobs according to a common metric. Recall that in Chapter One, we highlighted that one of the key strengths of economists' research on job quality was that it ranks jobs along a single continuum from 'lousy' to 'lovely' based on their average pay – and this was an attractive property of their method. It enabled them to chart the changing occupational structure and make statements about the evolution of 'job quality'. The key disadvantage, however, was that the ranking was based purely on a single dimension, pay, which we found in Chapter One to relate only weakly to job satisfaction once the other dimensions of job quality are entered into the equation.

This chapter introduces a method to meaningfully aggregate job quality dimensions together into a single metric, which it calls the Good Work Index (GWI). The proposed approach in fact takes inspiration from the mechanics underlying how inflation is calculated. One key challenge in creating any index is how to weight the various components going into it. One simple solution is to weight them all equally. This is clearly inadequate in the case of calculating inflation since we do not spend our incomes equally across different categories of goods and services. Changes in the cost of salt, for instance, only affect the overall cost of living very slightly, whereas changes in the cost of housing affect it much more. Inflation there-fore measures changes in prices based on a *weighted* basket of goods and services – with each category weighted according to how much the average household spends on it. Bigger ticket items affect inflation more than smaller ticket ones. The same differential weighting principle can be applied to calculating the GWI. We know from prior research (and the previous chapters) that different dimensions of the quality of work are not equally 'good'. For instance, the psychology research cited in Chapter One suggests that intrinsic features of work have a much larger effect on well-being than extrinsic factors. One solution might therefore be for the analyst to decide a priori what the (unequal) weight for each indicator should be based on this research.[1] Although this would satisfy the need to differentially weight, the choice of weights would clearly be arbitrary. This chapter argues that it should really be workers themselves who decide what is more and less important in defining weights. This chapter provides some evidence on and a solution to the weighting issue. It will then validate the resulting index in terms of its construct validity (to what extent it is predicted by the things we expect to predict it) and criterion validity (to what extent it predicts the things we expect it to predict). While we continue to use the SES in this chapter, the general principles of creating the GWI can be applied to any other datasets with appropriate job quality and job satisfaction measures. Further recommendations are saved for the final chapter.

Identifying indicators in the Skills and Employment Surveys

Before working out how to weight, the first step is identifying the ingredients, which the pervious chapter shed much light on. Turning to candidate indicators, we have trawled through the Skills and Employment questionnaires and picked out nine indicators from the SES which broadly correspond to most of the Carnegie's dimensions of Good Work. Our final indicators end up resembling those that the government will ultimately publish official statistics on,[2] though fewer in number given the data limitations of the SES and for definitional reasons. Notably excluded are both health, safety and psychosocial well-being, and social support and cohesion. Regarding the former, we do not include aspects of well-being in our job quality index since these are outcomes of job quality rather than a feature of the job. Regarding the latter, the SES unfortunately does not contain adequate indicators on this dimension.[3] Within the dimensions of Good Work, the SES also lacks certain indicators. For instance, we do not have data on hours insecurity, only job security.[4] We also would have liked more indicators on the dimensions for which we do have indicators, but alas we have to make do with what was there. The end result is that the ingredients to the GWI are tilted in favour of job design and the nature of work as the SES is very good on these. Nonetheless, it has an advantage in that our resulting index will be more a measure of work that offers realistic scope for development and fulfilment than of work that is decent and fair. While we know a great deal about how pay and security is stratified across the occupational structure, we know much less about how the more intrinsic aspects of work are stratified – and they may not necessarily coincide with the occupational pay and class structures.

In sifting through the literally dozens of candidate indicators, we also tried to identify indicators that go back as far as possible so that we can explore trends over time. Another consideration was identifying indicators that are fairly representative of the underlying domain. For instance, in the domain of consultative participation, we selected an item that asks whether management hold meetings where workers can express their views. This was preferred over another candidate item that asked whether a union or staff association existed at the workplace. Given these considerations, Table 3.1 lists the nine dimensions we arrived at as approximating Good Work:

1. Wages are measured in terms of hourly pay. The reason for looking at hourly pay rather than overall pay is that is standardizes for differences in hours worked.

2. Job security comes from a subjective measure. A potential issue is its subjective nature, although research has shown job security subjective indicators to be correlated with objective ones.[5] Another issue in relying on this indicator is that it notably does not include the topical issues of pay and hours insecurity (that is pay and hours varying from week to week or month to month in unpredictable ways). The exclusion of this type of insecurity is not to say it is not important. It is more a weakness of the current data. Nonetheless, the evidence suggests that forms of employment characterized by this (for example zero-hours contracts), though growing, still only cover a very small fraction of the labour market,[6] limiting the impact of the exclusion of this dimension on the overall picture.

3. Learning is captured by an item asking whether the job offers opportunities to learn new things. This taps into training and advancement opportunities too, but general enough to cover on-the-job learning.

4. A measure of skill-use. Good Work involves mastery and challenging work. This item is also broad enough to tap into over- and underemployment.

5. An index of task variety. This is central to job enlargement and job enrichment models where the goal was to decrease the routineness of work to keep it sufficiently interesting.
6. An index of task discretion. That is, the extent to which a worker can control their work tasks, also highlighted as important in the job characteristics models.
7. An indicator of job demands. An important consideration when selecting this item is that it refers to the requirements of the job, not how hard the person occupying it chooses to work as per our job-focus principle mentioned earlier.
8. Control over start and finishing times. An advantage of this item is that it is not referring to any specific flexibly policy – it is general enough to cover many. It is also about the control the worker has over work time, rather than whether hours simply vary.
9. Whether a worker has opportunities for participation. As mentioned earlier, an advantage of this indicator is that it covers a range of ways in which workers can have influence over organizational-level issues. This is particularly relevant to the self-employed who do not necessarily have a regular workplace, where the 'organization' is the customer or client.

Table 3.1: Indicators approximating Good Work

CIPD/Carnegie domains	Good Work indicators	Question wording	Coding scheme	Years available
Pay and benefits	Hourly pay	What is your usual gross pay before deductions for tax, national insurance and before any tax credits which you may receive? How many hours (per week) do you work for that pay?	Gross pay converted to weekly pay (deflated by the Consumer Price Index) then divided by usual number of hours per week. Then logarithm is taken.	1986, 1992, 1997, 2001, 2006, 2012, 2017
Terms of employment	Job security	Do you think there is any chance at all of you losing your job and becoming unemployed in the next twelve months? 1. Yes 2. No From this card, how would you rate the likelihood of this happening? 1. Very likely 2. Quite likely 3. Evens 4. Quite unlikely 5. Very unlikely	Coded ranging from 0 (very likely) to 4 (no chance).	1986, 1997, 2001, 2006, 2012, 2017

(continued)

Table 3.1: Indicators approximating Good Work (continued)

CIPD/Carnegie domains	Good Work indicators	Question wording	Coding scheme	Years available
Job design and the nature of work	Continuous learning	I am now going to read out a number of statements about your job. For each one, please tell me how much you agree or disagree with the statement: 'My job requires that I keep learning new things' 1. Strongly agree 2. Agree 3. Disagree 4. Strongly disagree	Coded ranging from 0 (strongly disagree) to 3 (strongly agree).	1992, 2001, 2006, 2012, 2017
	Skill-use opportunities	How much do you agree or disagree with the following statement: 'In my current job I have enough opportunity to use the knowledge and skills that I have' 1. Strongly agree 2. Agree 3. Disagree 4. Strongly disagree	Coded ranging from 0 (strongly disagree) to 3 (strongly agree).	2001, 2006, 2012, 2017

(continued)

Table 3.1: Indicators approximating Good Work (continued)

CIPD/Carnegie domains	Good Work indicators	Question wording	Coding scheme	Years available
	Task variety	How much variety is there in your job? Is there... 1. A great deal 2. Quite a lot 3. Some 4. A little 5. None at all	Coded ranging from 0 (none at all) to 3 (a great deal).	1997, 2001, 2006, 2012, 2017
	Task discretion	How much influence do you personally have on... 'how hard you work?' 'deciding what tasks you are to do?' 'deciding how you are to do the task?' 'deciding the quality standards to which you work?' 1. A great deal 2. A fair amount 3. Not much 4. None at all	The four items reverse coded ranging from 0 (not at all) to 3 (a great deal) and the respondent-specific mean from them is taken as an index.	1992, 1997, 2001, 2006, 2012, 2017

(continued)

Table 3.1: Indicators approximating Good Work (continued)

CIPD/Carnegie domains	Good Work indicators	Question wording	Coding scheme	Years available
	Job demands	I am now going to read out a number of statements about your job. For each one, please tell me how much you agree or disagree with the statement: 'My job requires that I work very hard' 1. Strongly agree 2. Agree 3. Disagree 4. Strongly disagree	Coded ranging from 0 (strongly disagree) to 3 (strongly agree).	1992, 1997, 2001, 2006, 2012, 2017
Work–life balance	Control over work time	How much do you agree or disagree with the following statement? 'I can decide the time I start and finish work' 1. Strongly agree 2. Agree 3. Disagree 4. Strongly disagree	Coded ranging from 0 (strongly disagree) to 3 (strongly agree).	2006, 2012, 2017

(continued)

Table 3.1: Indicators approximating Good Work (continued)

CIPD/Carnegie domains	Good Work indicators	Question wording	Coding scheme	Years available
Voice and representation	Participation opportunities	At your workplace, does management hold meetings in which you can express your views about what is happening in the organization? 1. Yes 2. No	Coded 1 (yes) and 0 (no).	1992, 1997, 2001, 2006, 2012, 2017

The Good Work Index

Now we can turn to how these indicators can be meaningfully summarized into a single index considering that not all aspects of work contribute equally to making work better or worse. Essentially, this is done by estimating a regression predicting overall job satisfaction and using the nine coefficients for each indicator as weights when summing how respondents' jobs score on these dimensions. More concretely, the following equation is estimated by OLS:

$$job\ satisfaction_i = \beta_1 job\ quality_{i1} + \beta_2 controls_{i2}$$

where $job\ quality_{i1}$ refers to a vector of the nine job quality dimensions (standardized using z-scores) and $controls_{i2}$ refer to a range of controls (survey year, gender, age, whether non-white ethnic group, whether have children, 11 UK regions, holding a degree-level qualification, whether part-time or full-time, whether self-employed or an employee, whether on a temporary or permanent contract, whether their workplace is unionized, three workplace size dummies, four industrial sector indicators, and 205 detailed occupational dummies).[7] Including the controls in this stage are important given that job quality and personal and work factors are likely to be correlated. Not including them could lead to spurious correlations between job quality and job satisfaction. For instance, suppose that those with children are more likely to seek out jobs with a higher degree of control over working time but that more satisfied people are also more likely to have children. Not considering whether someone has children or not would inflate the role of control over working time in predicting job satisfaction. The weights are therefore net of these sorts of confounding influences.

We obtain these coefficients from the pooled the 2006, 2012 and 2017 SES.[8] The nine job quality coefficients from this regression are then used to calculate a score for each job-quality dimension which is then summed for each respondent to calculate their overall GWI score. Table 3.2 illustrates how

Table 3.2: Good Work Index example

	β	$jobquality_{job1}$	$jobquality_{job2}$	β × job 1	β × job 2
Log hourly pay	0.002	3.458	2.700	0.007	0.005
Job security	0.143	6	4	0.858	0.572
Continuous learning	0.040	2	3	0.080	0.120
Skill-use	0.383	2	3	0.766	1.149
Task variety	0.194	3	4	0.582	0.776
Task discretion	0.226	2	3	0.452	0.678
Job demands	−0.027	2	1	−0.054	−0.027
Work time control	0.048	2	3	0.096	0.144
Participation opportunities	0.241	1	0	0.241	0.000
Good Work Index score				3.028	3.417

these scores are calculated for two example jobs. The weights (the βs) estimated in the equation are assumed to be the same for everyone, based on the previous analysis that shows there is not a great deal of difference in what makes work good across groups. As can be seen, job 1 is higher-paid and more secure than job 2. However, it scores less well in all other dimensions apart from job demands and participation opportunities. Since job 2 scores better in other dimensions, especially the crucial dimensions of skill-use, task variety and task discretion, it scores better overall. These scores are calculated for everybody in the SES sample.

The advantage of using the $\beta_1 \, job \, quality_{i1}$ coefficients as weights means there are no arbitrary decisions on behalf of the researchers in deciding how important different job quality dimensions are. Variants of this have been done before in prior research but are the exception rather than the norm.[9]

Summing up, the index is a combination of two elements: the (assumed) universal weights that each dimension of job quality has on job satisfaction multiplied by the extent to which these dimensions occur in a job. It thus informs us about the extent to which a job contains the elements known to augment job-related well-being and can then be used to rank jobs along a substantively meaningful continuum. While our main goal in developing the index is to map the overall hierarchy in the quality of jobs and occupations, this approach may well be useful to map year-to-year changes in overall job quality as it takes into consideration changing tastes and expectations of workers as well as actual changes in underlying job quality dimensions.[10] Clearly, all job quality dimensions should be mapped together. Relying on a single index alone can give a misleading picture given that dimensions may not always move in the same direction across time or between groups. As a single index, it is still an improvement on other existing approaches that use a single dimension of job quality, namely pay, or other indexing approaches that rely on arbitrary weighting schemes (if they weight at all). Having a single index is especially useful when exploring inequalities. The GWI can be aggregated up to explore disparities across occupations, as we do in the next chapter, or cities and regions, or whatever social grouping is of interest. It provides a simple meaningful ranking metric that gives each component its due weight in how it correlates with job satisfaction for the average worker.

There are other possible ways to rank jobs and occupations. One way might be to rank occupations by their job satisfaction. But as noted earlier, job satisfaction is not just about job quality – it can be influenced by many things, such as expectations and cognitive biases. Another way might be to take residual satisfaction across occupations net of controls in an OLS regression, as has been done in other research.[11] But then this will still be capturing other things not related directly to the job, things like social status and personal quirks that correlate with occupation.[12] This may be desirable for other purposes, but not specifically in our quest to develop a tool for mapping the job quality hierarchy. The advantage of the GWI over these approaches is that it conveys only information about job quality and not other unobserved factors. As we go on to show later, perhaps the biggest advantages of the GWI is that since we know what ingredients go into the GWI, it is possible to decompose differences in overall GWI scores across groups.

Before we present the results, we would like to stress that the GWI is limited by the available indicators in the SES. For instance, it does not take into account relations between colleagues, which is a fairly important dimension of job quality to workers. Nonetheless, we believe the principles behind the GWI – combining multiple job quality dimensions based on how much they relate to job satisfaction for the average worker – could be used to develop a national indicator. Just as cost of living changes are calculated based on a representative basket of goods and services weighted according to how much money people spend on them, such that changes in something that is common but expensive has bigger effects than an uncommon good that is cheap. Here the basket of goods are job qualities, and they are weighted according to the extent to which they relate to well-being. Like inflation, changes in GWI can be decomposed into changes according to how much people value different job qualities and changes in the underlying quantities themselves. To be clear, though, we see the main advantage of creating an overall index as being in its capacity to rank occupations along a meaningful metric – as an indicator of the structure of the *quality of work life chances* – that is the differential potential across occupations for fulfilment.

The characteristics of Good Work

A final step is to validate the GWI both in terms of construct and criterion validity. Taking construct validity first – ascertaining whether the things we expect to predict it actually predict it – Figures 3.1 and 3.2 report the results of the predictors from a single OLS regression but presents them in two separate graphs for ease of presentation. Taking what predicts GWI scores and work/workplace characteristics first, two main predictors stand out. First, occupational class. There are large differences in the average scores between managerial and professional occupations and manual and routine occupations, while jobs in intermediate occupations (largely clerical and technical support occupations) are around the median, on average. This quite clearly demonstrates occupational position is a big determinant of disparities. Second, employment status. Having a temporary contract is associated with much poorer job quality. Being self-employed, is associated with much higher job quality. This is largely because the self-employed score higher on the intrinsic dimensions, which weigh heavily in determining GWI scores. Part-time jobs are generally poorer than full-time ones, while those in the public sector are on average better than those in other sectors, whose job quality in turn is about average. Perhaps surprisingly, there are no noticeable differences across categories of workplace size nor between unionized and non-unionized workplaces net of the other factors.

Figure 3.1: Predicted average GWI percentile by work characteristics

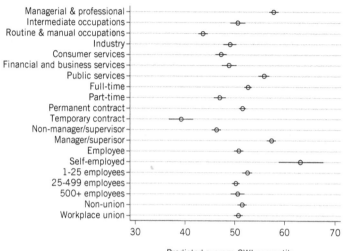

Predicted average GWI percentile

Notes: All workers aged 2v0 to 60 in the Skills and Employment Surveys 2006, 2012 and 2017. Data are weighted. Model includes controls for survey year, gender, age, whether non-white ethnic group, whether have children, 11 UK regions, holding a degree-level qualification, whether part-time or full-time, whether self-employed or an employee, whether on a temporary or permanent contract, whether their workplace is unionized, three workplace size dummies, four industrial sector indicators, and occupational class dummies. Horizontal lines are 95% confidence intervals.

Turning to socio-demographic predictors, unsurprisingly, graduates enjoy better jobs and there is an age gradient, with younger workers tending to work in lower-quality jobs and graduates tend to have better-quality jobs. Perhaps surprisingly, there is little difference between the genders on average. However, there is a large ethnic penalty – which is a cause for concern that we previously did not know existed. Those identifying as belonging to non-white ethnic groups tend to occupy jobs with quality below the median on average. Interestingly, job quality in London is significantly below other regions, while in Wales it is highest. Further analysis reveals

Figure 3.2: Predicted average GWI percentile by worker characteristics

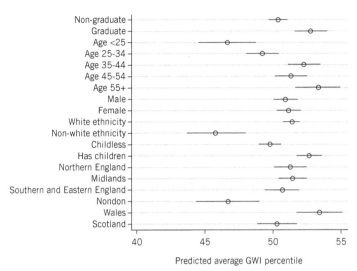

Predicted average GWI percentile

Notes: All workers aged 20 to 60 in the Skills and Employment Surveys 2006, 2012 and 2017. Data are weighted. Model includes controls for survey year, gender, age, whether non-white ethnic group, whether have children, 11 UK regions, holding a degree-level qualification, whether part-time or full-time, whether self-employed or an employee, whether on a temporary or permanent contract, whether their workplace is unionized, three workplace size dummies, four industrial sector indicators, and occupational class dummies. Horizontal lines are 95% confidence intervals.

this is because Londoners report lowest task variety and job security on average, while workers in Wales report the highest levels of skill-use.

Is Good Work good for you?

The next validation step is to demonstrate that the GWI predicts what it has been designed to predict (criterion validity). Is Good Work good for workers? We explore how

Figure 3.3: GWI decile and affective well-being

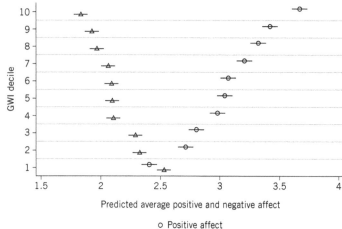

Predicted average positive and negative affect

o Positive affect
△ Negative affect

Notes: All workers aged 20 to 60 in the Skills and Employment Surveys 2006, 2012 and 2017. Data are weighted. Model includes controls for survey year, gender, age, whether non-white ethnic group, whether have children, 11 UK regions, holding a degree-level qualification, whether part-time or full-time, whether self-employed or an employee, whether on a temporary or permanent contract, whether their workplace is unionized, three workplace size dummies, four industrial sector indicators, and occupational class dummies. Positive and negative affect are measured using Warr's scales of job-related affect. Horizontal lines are 95% confidence intervals.

job quality predicts affective well-being, job attitudes and life satisfaction. To simplify presentation, GWI scores have been collapsed into deciles. These demonstrate that scoring higher on the GWI is associated with lower negative affect and higher positive affect (Figure 3.3), higher commitment and greater discretionary effort (Figure 3.4), and higher life satisfaction (Figure 3.5).[13] Overall, then, Good Work as measured by the GWI is associated with better well-being measured in a few ways. What is especially revealing by these figures is the effect is not linear. Those in the lowest decile fare particularly worse even when compared to those in the

Figure 3.4: GWI decile and job attitudes

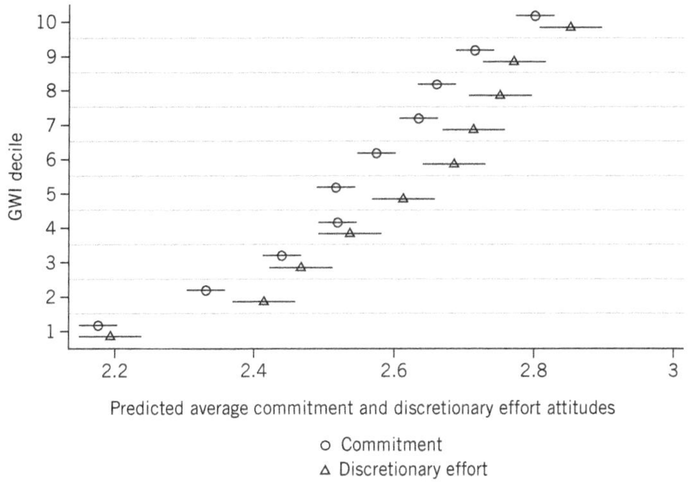

Predicted average commitment and discretionary effort attitudes

○ Commitment
△ Discretionary effort

Notes: All workers aged 20 to 60 in the Skills and Employment Surveys 2006, 2012 and 2017. Data are weighted. Model includes controls for survey year, gender, age, whether non-white ethnic group, whether have children, 11 UK regions, holding a degree-level qualification, whether part-time or full-time, whether self-employed or an employee, whether on a temporary or permanent contract, whether their workplace is unionized, three workplace size dummies, four industrial sector indicators, and occupational class dummies. Horizontal lines are 95% confidence intervals.

decile just above, especially with respect to job attitudes and life satisfaction.

Summary and conclusions

- The GWI is a summary indicator based on nine indicators of job quality (wages, job security, continuous learning requirements, skill-use opportunities, task variety, task discretion, job demands, control over working time, and participation opportunities) – with each component weighted according to how much it influences job satisfaction for the

Figure 3.5: GWI decile and life satisfaction

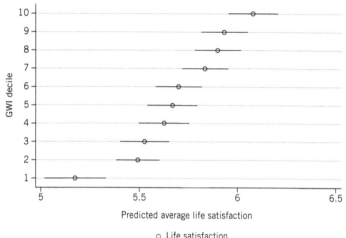

Predicted average life satisfaction

o Life satisfaction

Notes: All workers aged 20 to 60 in the Skills and Employment Survey 2017. Data are weighted. Model includes controls for survey year, gender, age, whether non-white ethnic group, whether have children, 11 UK regions, holding a degree-level qualification, whether part-time or full-time, whether self-employed or an employee, whether on a temporary or permanent contract, whether their workplace is unionized, three workplace size dummies, four industrial sector indicators, and occupational class dummies. Horizontal lines are 95% confidence intervals.

average worker. In line with decades of prior research, we find factors related to the nature of work weigh more heavily in determining the well-being potential of jobs relative to more extrinsic factors like pay.

• Using the GWI to define the job quality hierarchy, we find that managerial and professional occupations have the best job quality on average, with manual and routine occupations having the worst, and intermediate occupations in the middle. There are no noticeable differences across categories of workplace size nor between unionized and non-unionized workplaces. Perhaps surprisingly, there is little difference between the genders on average. However, worryingly, we find a large ethnic job quality penalty.

- Overall job quality is associated with more positive affect, lower negative affect, more positive job attitudes and higher life satisfaction. Importantly, these effects tend to be non-linear. The negative effects of very low-quality work is bigger than the positive effects of high-quality work.

FOUR

The Occupational Quality Structure

Introduction

Having created the GWI, this chapter explores disparities in the quality of work life chances across the occupational structure given the emphasis placed on enduring occupational disparities in life chances by stratification research in sociology. An occupational approach can be useful in situations where occupation data is available but not job quality information. The goal of this chapter is to identify the occupational quality structure. It does it in two ways. First, it examines the distribution of overall job quality as proxied by the GWI across the class structure. Second, it compares the pattern of disparities in the GWI and that of pay across occupational categories, which reveals both significant overlaps and many interesting exceptions.

Good Work across the class structure

One way social scientists convey complex multidimensional phenomena is with classifications. While it is generally taken as a given in sociology that one's occupation – or field of work – is critical to a whole range of life outcomes, and not just those related to work and economic life,[1] how best to classify occupations to meaningful groups is quite contested. In fact, there has been a whole industry in the discipline of sociology that has devoted itself to lively and often heated debates in this regard. These debates will not be summarized here, if only because they have been treated very comprehensively elsewhere and the substance of the debates never really changes.[2]

A common strand within stratification research is around the notion of socio-economic classes – broad and durable groupings of individuals that share broadly similar life chances. Such groupings are often aggregated classifications of very detailed occupational categories found in social surveys. Perhaps the most influential occupational classification in the UK context and Europe is that associated with John Goldthorpe and colleagues. It followed a long lineage of British social mobility studies mapping the (un)changing relationship between parental and offspring socio-economic classes. In this tradition, broad groupings of occupations (classes) are taken as indicators of position within wider socio-economic hierarchies. The classifications used in these studies were often piecemeal and lacked a sound theoretical basis. It was uncertain how valid an indicator they were as indicators of socio-economic position. This culminated in the development of the bespoke National Statistics Socio-economic Classification (NS-SEC) by the ONS, which also included a raft of validation studies.[3] NS-SEC has been around since the early 2000s and is the government's official socio-economic indicator, used in the census and other official statistics. A similar classification based on NS-SEC was later developed and validated by the same team for European statistical agencies.[4]

The theoretical basis to the NS-SEC schema is that differences in employment relations underlying socio-economic classes give rise to differences in the life chances across classes. The specific theoretical basis combines some of the Marxian notions about relations to the means of production (distinctions between employers, employees and the self-employed) with Weberian notions of inequality in economic life chances between different grades of employees (occupations vary in the extent to which they require specialist skills and the extent to which employers can dictate the terms) in denoting socio-economic positions.[5] Empirically, it allocates respondents in surveys to seven classes based on a combination of their occupation, employment status and supervision duties.[6] Table 4.1 lists the seven NS-SEC categories, their typical employment relations and the largest occupations within each category, as well as the broad classes to which each belongs.

The other main way of classifying occupations in surveys is according to the broad field of work combined with broad skill-level required, that is, the required qualifications and training routes (including how long it typically takes to progress to that level through training or experience). The ONS classifies occupations according to SOC codes in this way based on the respondents' job title and a brief description they give of their main duties. These detailed codes can be aggregated up to nine SOC 'major' categories: (1) managerial occupations; (2) professional occupations; (3) associate professional occupations; (4) administrative and secretarial occupations; (5) skilled trades; (6) personal services; (7) sales and customer services; (8) process, plant and machine operatives; and (9) elementary occupations.[7] ISCO – an international occupational classification used across countries is based on similar principles and has a similar hierarchical structure and groupings.[8]

For the purposes of mapping job quality across broad occupational groups, NS-SEC is preferred for several reasons. First, it has a sound theoretical basis relevant to the purposes of mapping disparities in the quality of working life. Classes not only represent broad differences in employment relations, but also differences in underlying skills and tasks (and their prices) and authority relations within the workplace. These all have direct theoretical connections with the Good Work dimensions (Table 3.1). Second, the NS-SEC is both widely used and well validated for mapping social disparities at work.[9]

How might this model of occupational class be extended to the quality of work life chances? Viewing the occupational

Table 4.1: NS-SEC categories

Big class (3 classes)	NS-SEC (7 classes)	Employment relations	Largest five occupations in the SES
Managerial and professional occupations	Higher managerial and professional occupations (including large employers)	Service relationship	Software professionals; financial managers and chartered secretaries; marketing and sales managers (large employers); scientific researchers; management consultants, actuaries, economists and statisticians
	Lower managerial and professional occupations	Service relationship	Nurses; primary and nursery education teaching professionals; secondary education teaching professionals; marketing and sales managers (small employers); retail and wholesale managers
Intermediate occupations	Intermediate occupations	Mixed	General office assistants/clerks; accounts and wages clerks, book-keepers, other financial clerks; customer care occupations; nursing auxiliaries and assistants; Civil Service administrative officers and assistants

(continued)

Table 4.1: NS-SEC categories (continued)

Big class (3 classes)	NS-SEC (7 classes)	Employment relations	Largest five occupations in the SES
	Small employers and own-account workers	Mixed	Carpenters and joiners; bricklayers, masons; electricians, electrical fitters; painters and decorators; glaziers, window fabricators and fitters
Routine and manual occupations	Lower supervisory and lower technical occupations	Labour contract (modified)	Metal working production and maintenance fitters (supervisor); sales and retail assistants (supervisor); care assistants and home carers (supervisor); electricians, electrical fitters (supervisor); routine inspectors and testers
	Semi-routine occupations	Labour contract	Sales and retail assistants; care assistants and home carers; educational assistants kitchen and catering assistants; retail cashiers and check-out operators
	Routine occupations	Labour contract	Cleaners, domestics; heavy goods vehicle drivers; other goods handling and storage occupations; van drivers; bar staff

Notes: Adapted from Williams (2017b). Data are weighted.

structure in this way, we would expect individuals in managerial and professional occupations to have the highest GWI scores and routine and manual ones to have the lowest. Making it into this class is the measure of success in social mobility and occupational attainment studies. It is more open where the intermediate occupations should fall. How job quality defined more broadly than by economic prospects is structured by occupational class has been less studied. As NS-SEC categories may obscure deeper structures of inequality within classes, it is also necessary to examine the pattern at the most detailed level of occupational classification.

Figure 4.1 compares the mean percentile position of occupations in the GWI and the pay hierarchies by NS-SEC category. One reason for converting GWI scores and pay to percentiles for this analysis is that they are measured on different

Figure 4.1: Mean percentile position of the GWI and hourly pay by NS-SEC

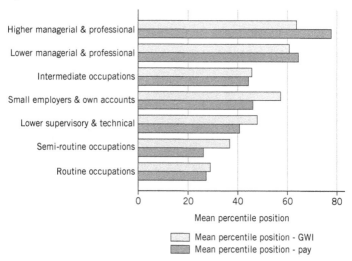

Notes: All workers aged 20 to 60 in the Skills and Employment Surveys 2006, 2012 and 2017. Data are weighted.

scales. Taking percentiles effectively puts them on the same scale. We find that managerial and professional occupations have the highest pay, and semi-routine and routine occupations have the lowest pay, with the other three classes in between. While GWI scores broadly follow a similar class-based hierarchy, small employer and own-account workers stand out as having almost similar average GWI percentile positions to lower managerial and professional occupations. The other stand-out finding is that non-managerial and professional occupations tend to have higher average GWI scores than their pay alone might suggest, while the opposite is the case for managerial and professional occupations.

To look at the pattern from a different angle, Figure 4.2 divides the labour force into three equal-sized groups according to GWI scores and then plots the proportion of workers in each

Figure 4.2: Fraction of each NS-SEC category in the top, middle and bottom thirds of the Good Work hierarchy

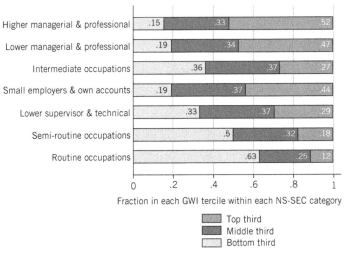

Fraction in each GWI tercile within each NS-SEC category

Top third
Middle third
Bottom third

Notes: All workers aged 20 to 60 in the Skills and Employment Surveys 2006, 2012 and 2017. Data are weighted.

class within each of these three groups. Two things stand out from this figure. First, that small employers and own-account workers – though conventionally considered intermediate classes in the NS-SEC hierarchy – have comparable (though slightly lower) chances of being in the top third of the GWI distribution to managerial and professional occupations. Second, intermediate occupations have higher chances of being in the bottom third of the GWI distribution than lower supervisory and technical occupations, which are considered in the bottom class of routine and manual occupations in the three-category version of NS-SEC.

In short, these two exercises demonstrate that the class ordering of the Good Work structure is somewhat different to the pay structure, namely in between the extremes. While the pay hierarchy runs more or less as in Table 4.1, the job quality hierarchy runs from higher managerial and professional, lower managerial and professional, small employers and own-account workers, lower supervisory and technical occupations, intermediate occupations, semi-routine occupations and routine occupations.

Although the main advantage of the GWI is that it combines multiple dimensions of job quality together into a single index, a potential disadvantage of this is that it might obscure *why* differences between groups are as they are. For instance, why is that semi-routine and routine occupations have much lower GWI scores than higher managerial and professional occupations? To answer such questions, we can easily decompose GWI differences. Recall from Chapter Three that GWI scores are simply the weighted sum of the nine Good Work dimensions (weighted by their partial correlation with overall job satisfaction – see Table 3.2 for the specific weights). This means the average GWI scores of a group (such as an NS-SEC category) are additively decomposable into these constituent components.[10] In other words, we can apportion differences in GWI scores across groups to differences in the specific underlying Good Work dimensions.

Table 4.2: Weighted means of Good Work dimensions by NS-SEC

	HM&P	LM&P	IO	SE&OA	LS&T	S-RO	RO
GWI score	3.201	3.143	2.849	3.115	2.873	2.610	2.432
Pay	0.006	0.005	0.005	0.005	0.005	0.004	0.004
Security	0.765	0.776	0.775	0.794	0.769	0.768	0.755
Learning	0.096	0.094	0.084	0.084	0.083	0.073	0.061
Skill-use	0.946	0.912	0.816	0.931	0.843	0.755	0.712
Variety	0.632	0.615	0.520	0.599	0.526	0.444	0.390
Discretion	0.540	0.547	0.490	0.606	0.520	0.447	0.432
Demands	−0.064	−0.066	−0.060	−0.066	−0.061	−0.058	−0.057
Work time	0.091	0.069	0.058	0.108	0.039	0.034	0.038
Participation	0.188	0.190	0.161	0.055	0.149	0.142	0.096

Notes: All workers aged 20 to 60 in the Skills and Employment Surveys 2006, 2012 and 2017. HM&P = higher managerial and professional; LM&P = lower managerial and professional; SE&OA = small employers and own accounts; LS&T = lower supervisory and technical; S-RO = semi-routine occupations; RO = routine occupations.

Table 4.2 gives the weighted Good Work dimension scores by NS–SEC (that is, the β weights in Table 3.2 multiplied by the means of each underlying Good Work dimension for each NS–SEC). NS–SEC-specific GWI scores are simply the sum of these. The information in Table 4.2 is then used to calculate differences in each cell relative to the higher managerial and professional class in Table 4.3. In principle, the reference class can be set to any class and the procedure is otherwise the same. We set the reference class to higher managerial and professional occupations here simply because they have the highest average GWI score so we can find out why other classes score worse.

Table 4.3 demonstrates that semi–routine and routine occupations have 0.591 and 0.769 lower average GWI scores than higher managerial and professional occupations and that this is largely accounted for by their inferior skill-use, task variety and task discretion. These three factors alone account for roughly 30, 30 and 15 per cent respectively of the gaps with

Table 4.3: Decomposing differences in GWI scores by NS-SEC

	HM&P	LM&P	IO	SE&OA	LS&T	S-RO	RO
GWI score	0	−0.057	−0.352	−0.085	−0.327	−0.591	−0.769
Pay	0	−0.001	−0.001	−0.001	−0.001	−0.002	−0.002
Security	0	0.011	0.010	0.029	0.004	0.003	−0.010
Learning	0	−0.002	−0.013	−0.013	−0.013	−0.023	−0.035
Skill-use	0	−0.034	−0.130	−0.015	−0.103	−0.192	−0.234
Variety	0	−0.017	−0.113	−0.033	−0.107	−0.188	−0.243
Discretion	0	0.007	−0.050	0.066	−0.020	−0.093	−0.108
Demands	0	−0.002	0.004	−0.002	0.003	0.006	0.007
Work time	0	−0.022	−0.033	0.017	−0.051	−0.057	−0.053
Participation	0	0.002	−0.027	−0.133	−0.039	−0.046	−0.092

Notes: All workers aged 20 to 60 in the Skills and Employment Surveys 2006, 2012 and 2017. HM&P = higher managerial and professional; LM&P = lower managerial and professional; SE&OA = small employers and own accounts; LS&T = lower supervisory and technical; S-RO = semi-routine occupations; RO = routine occupations.

higher managerial and professional occupations – collectively explaining more than 75 per cent of the gaps in GWI scores. While pay inequalities between these groups are well known, what is interesting about these findings is that class inequality extends to job quality defined more broadly.

We can also explore in a bit more detail the interesting cases of small employers and own-account workers and intermediate occupations. Relative to higher managerial and professional occupations, small employers and own-account workers have higher task discretion, greater job security and greater control over work time. In many ways, this is unsurprising. It quite clearly demonstrates some of the intrinsic benefits of being self-employed – freeing oneself from the shackles of an employer to gain greater control over one's work life and security, even if it means accepting lower and possibly more volatile pay. Moving onto the other interesting case of intermediate occupations,

even though this is a non-manual group, they have significantly lower skill-use, task variety and task discretion than
higher managerial and professional occupations – and indeed
are lower than those of the lower supervisory and technical
group – a manual group.

Taken together, what these exercises demonstrate is that the
class structure in terms of overall job quality (as captured by
the GWI and its components) is somewhat similar but different
from the class structure in terms of economic life prospects
(as captured by looking at pay). While both have managerial
and professional occupations and semi-routine and routine
occupations at the extremes, the evidence presented here is that
in the middle of the class structure, things are quite different.
This has implications for reducing the more detailed seven
classes to a smaller number of big classes, which is often done
when the NS-SEC schema is applied in sociological studies
(such as social mobility studies). While the seven NS-SEC
categories are normally reduced to three big classes by combining the two managerial ones together, combining intermediate and small employers and own-account workers into
a second intermediate category, and lower supervisory and
technical, semi-routine and routine into a third routine and
manual category – the evidence presented here is that small
employers and own-account workers are not so intermediate
in terms of satisfaction potential. Although speculative, and
in need of further validation and scrutiny, a possible way of
how NS-SEC categories might be regrouped and reordered in
class-based research in terms of overall job quality as opposed
to economic prospects is given in Table 4.4. This would be
useful in revaluating social mobility studies from an overall job
quality perspective, for example.

Small employers and own-account workers are mostly
composed of semi-routine and routine occupations that are
self-employed and employ fewer than 25 workers. Quite
clearly, then, one route to improving overall job quality in such
occupations is to go self-employed and turn your craft into a

Table 4.4: The possible Good Work class hierarchy redrawn in terms of job satisfaction potential

Possible big class label	NS-SEC	Core features
High-satisfaction potential occupations	Higher managerial and professional occupations (including large employers)	High skill-use, task variety and work time control
	Lower managerial and professional occupations	
	Small employers and own-account workers	
Moderate-satisfaction potential occupations	Lower supervisory and lower technical occupations	Moderate skill-use, task variety and work time control
	Intermediate occupations	
Low-satisfaction potential occupations	Semi-routine occupations	Low skill-use, task variety and work time control
	Routine occupations	

business. Similarly, lower supervisory and technical occupations are largely composed of semi-routine and routine occupations with the main exception being they are supervisors. Again, having more authority within the workplace is associated with higher overall job quality than being a non-supervisory employee within these occupations. These findings echo the findings in Figure 3.1 which showed that self-employment and having managerial duties are associated with higher GWI scores.

Although classes are a fundamental unit of analysis in stratification research, one persistent criticism of them is that they can obscure within-class differences. There is probably substantial variation between the micro-classes or occupations that make up classes. Indeed, when we look at the differences in average GWI scores between the within-class 20th percentile to the within-class 80th percentile in Figure 4.3, we find that within-class inequality in GWI scores is greatest in semi-routine and routine occupations.

Figure 4.3: Ratio of within-class P80 to P20 GWI scores and hourly pay

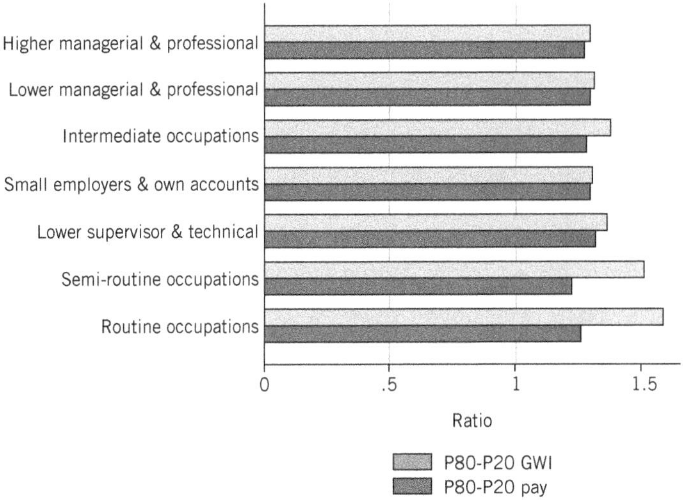

Ratio

- P80-P20 GWI
- P80-P20 pay

Notes: All workers aged 20 to 60 in the Skills and Employment Surveys 2006, 2012 and 2017.

The job at the 80th percentile within both these classes has on average a GWI score around 1.5 times higher than the job at the 20th percentile within these classes, whereas for other classes the gap is lower, around 1.25 times higher. Other weighs of calculating within-class inequality in GWI scores showed a similar pattern.[11] This greater gap between the worst and the best jobs within the semi-routine and routine classes indicates there is greater scope for improvement here. It highlights the potentially greater role of the workplace for improving the quality of jobs in such occupations. Interestingly, when it comes to pay, within-class inequalities are fairly constant across classes.

The steeper gradient in pay across classes and the constant within-class inequality in pay implies class is a better predictor of pay than overall job quality. Overall, though, class is still a reasonable approximation of disparities in overall job quality. It is just the class ordering in the middle may be a bit different.

Comparing the occupational quality and occupational-pay structures

As the previous figure revealed, there could be important differences between occupations within classes. There is a long-standing debate in sociology on the shape of the class structure, whether inequalities are best conceptualized in terms of classes or micro-classes, that is, aggregations of occupations into a handful of categories versus hundreds of categories.[12] It is therefore useful to look at detailed occupations directly to spot interesting exceptions in any case. Figure 4.4 plots occupational mean GWI scores against occupational mean pay. In general, higher-paying occupations score better on the GWI. We would expect a positive correlation since pay is one ingredient of the GWI, albeit one that affects it not very much relative to the other ingredients (see Table 3.2). Unsurprisingly, then, excluding pay from the GWI results in an almost identical graph (not shown). What is also interesting is that the spread broadly corresponds to big classes,

Figure 4.4: Occupational GWI scores by occupational pay

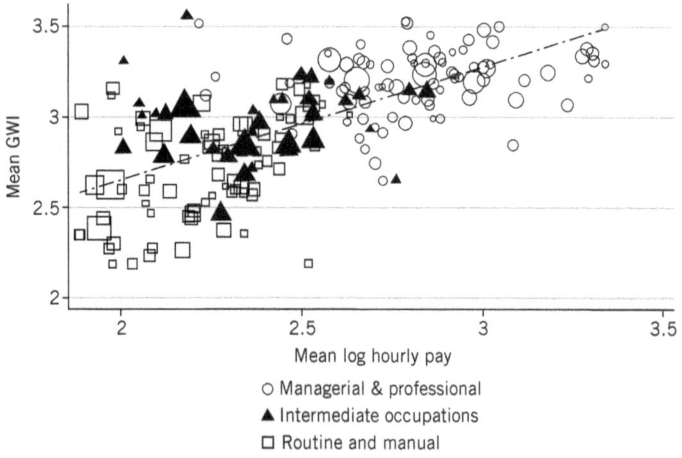

Notes: All workers aged 20 to 60 in the Skills and Employment Surveys 2006, 2012 and 2017.

though there is certainly overlap in the middle. Again, this is not surprising given the previous analysis, which highlighted small employers and own-account workers as standing out from other intermediate occupations. A final interesting observation from this figure concerns lower-paying occupations. As there is much greater variation in the GWI scores of the lowest-paid occupations compared to the very high-paying ones. This reinforces the finding from Figure 4.3 that there is greater variation in the quality of work at the lower end of the labour market, implying there is scope here for workplaces to (probably only modestly) improve overall job quality.

Another advantage of exploring detailed occupations is that we can go one step further and identify specific occupations. This is useful to see the best and the worst occupations as well as to see interesting extreme exceptions to the class theme, as well as interesting extreme cases more generally.

Table 4.5 lists the 20 occupations with the highest GWI scores. It also lists their average GWI and hourly pay per-centile positions. According to the GWI, product and fashion designers have the highest overall job quality. Interestingly, this is classified as an intermediate occupation in NS-SEC, while the rest of the top 20 are all managerial and profes-sional occupations.[13] Moving onto the bottom 20 (Table 4.6), except for call-centre workers, all the occupations belong to the semi-routine and routine classes. In the middle (Table 4.7), the specific occupations are drawn evenly from man-agerial and professional, intermediate, and manual and routine occupations. These three tables reinforce the conclusions from the previous exercises showing that the extremes of the Good Work spectrum are fairly well segregated according to class, while things get a bit more complicated in the middle.

One advantage of not relying on coarse class schemas and really drilling down to the detailed occupational level is that we can identify the many occupations where their GWI score is much higher or lower than if we defined occupational quality in terms of just pay, as was observed in Figure 4.4.

Table 4.5: Top 20 occupations by mean GWI score

Detailed occupation	Mean GWI percentile	Mean hourly pay percentile
Product, clothing and related designers	82.1	54.8
Chartered surveyors (not quantity surveyors)	79.5	75.9
Occupational therapists	79.2	73.8
Clergy	78.8	84.6
Officers in armed forces / police officers (inspectors and above)*	78.2	32.4
Directors and chief executives of major organizations / senior officials in national government*	78.1	96.2
Higher education teaching professionals	77.4	81.7
Physiotherapists/chiropodists*	76.1	70.4
Hotel and accommodation managers	75.1	25.7
Managers in construction / managers in mining and energy*	74.9	79.8
Personnel, training and industrial relations managers	73.0	78.6
Residential and day care managers	72.8	56.8
Civil engineers / mechanical engineers / electrical engineers / electronics engineers / chemical engineers*	71.6	77.0
Medical practitioners	71.1	70.6
Purchasing managers	71.0	82.6
Scientific researchers / social science researchers / researchers n.e.c.*	70.8	89.1
Management consultants, actuaries, economists and statisticians	70.4	85.9

(continued)

Table 4.5: Top 20 occupations by mean GWI score (continued)

Detailed occupation	Mean GWI percentile	Mean hourly pay percentile
Social services managers	70.2	71.6
Farm managers / natural environment and conservation managers / managers in animal husbandry, forestry and fishing n.e.c.*	69.8	58.1
Financial managers and chartered secretaries	69.1	87.0

Notes: All workers aged 20 to 60 in the Skills and Employment Surveys 2006, 2012 and 2017.
* Denotes occupational unit group has been merged with another or multiple unit groups to increase cell size.
n.e.c. = not elsewhere classified

For instance, there are quite a few relatively high-paying occupations like solicitors, production engineers, and senior educational administrators and inspectors. Workers in these occupations are on average in the top third of the overall pay distribution, but the average potential for high overall job quality in their jobs is middling. There are also occupations that have middling overall job quality, but they are low paid. Examples include educational assistants, nursery nurses, chefs and window cleaners – each with their pay in the bottom third of the pay distribution.

These sorts of 'exceptional' occupations can be identified more generally throughout the occupational structure by subtracting the average occupational GWI percentile positions from average occupational pay percentile positions. Table 4.8 lists the top 20 occupations with the largest positive gap between the two indicators, while Table 4.9 lists the top 20 with the largest negative gap. These two tables nicely illustrate an advantage of the GWI over class-based approaches to mapping stratification in Good Work: we can identify specific occupations and group them in ways that may not be readily apparent by focusing

Table 4.6: Bottom 20 occupations by mean GWI score

Detailed occupation	Mean GWI percentile	Mean hourly pay percentile
Elementary personal services occupations n.e.c. / hospital porters / hotel porters*	31.8	21.4
Food, drink and tobacco process operatives	31.3	36.7
Elementary sales occupations n.e.c.	29.6	31.6
Other goods handling and storage occupations n.e.c. / stevedores, dockers and slingers*	29.4	29.6
Call-centre agents / operators	28.9	24.8
Bus and coach drivers	28.1	32.1
Assemblers (vehicles and metal goods) / assemblers (electrical products) / tyre, exhaust and windscreen fitters*	28.0	39.7
Traffic wardens	25.7	24.5
Cleaners, domestics	24.5	15.7
Postal workers, mail sorters, messengers, couriers	24.1	40.7
Telephonists / Market research interviewers*	23.5	15.6
Waiters, waitresses	22.9	19.3
Retail cashiers and check-out operators	22.6	12.0
Shelf fillers	22.4	39.1
Bar staff	22.1	37.0
Van drivers	22.1	27.0
Packers, bottlers, canners, fillers	21.6	10.2
Launderers, dry cleaners, pressers	21.3	19.6
Textiles, garments and related trades n.e.c. / weavers and knitters / upholsterers / leather and related trades / tailors and dressmakers*	21.1	18.0
Driving instructors	13.1	42.0

Notes: All workers aged 20 to 60 in the Skills and Employment Surveys 2006, 2012 and 2017.
* Denotes occupational unit group has been merged with another or multiple unit groups to increase cell size.
n.e.c. = not elsewhere classified

Table 4.7: Middle 20 occupations by mean GWI score

Detailed occupation	Mean GWI percentile	Mean hourly pay percentile
Educational assistants	55.3	29.4
Chartered and certified accountants	55.0	74.3
Retail and wholesale managers	54.6	42.2
Tool makers, tool fitters and markers-out	54.2	58.9
Solicitors and lawyers, judges and coroners / legal professionals n.e.c.*	53.7	83.6
Nursery nurses	52.4	21.4
Metal working production and maintenance fitters	52.4	57.7
Library assistants / clerks	52.3	45.3
Caretakers	52.3	39.7
Chefs, cooks	51.8	28.1
Journalists, newspaper and periodical editors	51.6	58.8
Ambulance staff (excluding paramedics)	51.1	48.6
Vehicle body builders and repairers	51.1	53.2
Local government clerical officers and assistants	50.9	59.1
Engineering professionals n.e.c.	50.8	71.7
Registrars and senior administrators of educational establishments / education officers, school inspectors*	50.0	69.4
Production and process engineers / planning and quality control engineers*	49.9	67.1
Carpenters and joiners	49.6	46.3
Transport operatives n.e.c. / rail transport operatives / seafarers (merchant navy); barge, lighter and boat operatives / air transport operatives*	49.0	49.7
Window cleaners	49.0	33.4

Notes: All workers aged 20 to 60 in the Skills and Employment Surveys 2006, 2012 and 2017.
* Denotes occupational unit group has been merged with another or multiple unit groups to increase cell size.
n.e.c. = not elsewhere classified

Table 4.8: Top 20 occupations where average GWI percentile position is greater than average pay percentile position ('artisan occupations')

Detailed occupation	Difference	Mean GWI percentile	Mean hourly pay percentile
Beauticians and related occupations	−55.1	66.9	11.9
Hotel and accommodation managers	−49.4	75.1	25.7
Clergy	−45.8	78.2	32.4
Leisure and theme park attendants	−45.3	57.0	11.7
Hairdressers, barbers	−44.7	58.7	14.1
Playgroup leaders/assistants	−35.8	55.2	19.3
Publicans and managers of licensed premises	−32.1	61.3	29.2
Nursery nurses	−31.0	52.4	21.4
Bakers, flour confectioners	−27.9	47.9	20.1
Product, clothing and related designers	−27.3	82.1	54.8
Educational assistants	−26.0	55.3	29.4
Restaurant and catering managers	−25.4	57.2	31.8
School secretaries	−24.5	57.2	32.6
Chefs, cooks	−23.7	51.8	28.1
Care assistants and home carers	−21.6	46.9	25.3
Kitchen and catering assistants	−20.1	34.1	14.0
Dispensing opticians	−17.8	55.2	37.4
Receptionists	−17.8	44.2	26.4
Sales and retail assistants	−17.7	34.3	16.6
Leisure and travel service occupations n.e.c.	−17.3	45.5	28.2

Notes: All workers aged 20 to 60 in the Skills and Employment Surveys 2006, 2012 and 2017.
* Denotes occupational unit group has been merged with another or multiple unit groups to increase cell size.
n.e.c. = not elsewhere classified

Table 4.9: Top 20 occupations where average GWI percentile position is less than average pay percentile position ('routine professional occupations')

Detailed occupation	Difference	Mean GWI percentile	Mean hourly pay percentile
Aircraft pilots and flight engineers / air traffic controllers / ship and hovercraft officers / train drivers*	42.9	41.2	84.1
Solicitors and lawyers, judges and coroners / legal professionals n.e.c.*	30.0	53.7	83.6
Computer engineers, installation and maintenance	29.9	40.3	69.6
Financial and accounting technicians	25.7	47.9	73.6
Software professionals	23.4	56.0	79.4
Non-commissioned officers and other ranks	22.0	42.8	64.8
Financial institution managers	21.7	61.8	83.5
Information and communication technology managers	21.1	61.8	83.5
Architectural technologists and town planning technicians / building and civil engineering technicians*	21.0	48.7	70.0
Engineering professionals n.e.c.	20.9	50.8	71.7
Estimators, valuers and assessors	20.4	36.0	56.3
Registrars and senior administrators of educational establishments / education officers, school inspectors*	19.3	50.0	69.4
Taxation experts	19.3	66.2	85.6
Chartered and certified accountants / management accountants*	19.2	55.0	74.3
Architects	18.9	65.8	84.7
Psychologists	18.4	66.2	84.6

(continued)

Table 4.9: Top 20 occupations where average GWI percentile position is less than average pay percentile position ('routine professional occupations') (continued)

Detailed occupation	Difference	Mean GWI percentile	Mean hourly pay percentile
Medical practitioners	18.4	66.2	84.6
Directors and chief executives of major organizations / senior officials in national government*	18.1	78.1	96.2
Financial managers and chartered secretaries	17.9	69.1	87.0
IT strategy and planning professionals	17.3	68.3	85.6

Notes: All workers aged 20 to 60 in the Skills and Employment Surveys 2006, 2012 and 2017.
* Denotes occupational unit group has been merged with another or multiple unit groups to increase cell size.
n.e.c. = not elsewhere classified

on pay or class alone. For instance, one would not normally think beauticians, clergy, product and fashion designers, nursery nurses, pub landlords and bakers having much in common! What they share is that their potential overall job quality is much higher than their relative potential for paying well. By contrast, the other group is exclusively composed of professional occupations, most being related to finance, law and information technology.[14] In general, these are some of the most highly paid occupations – in a sense giving them more scope for their average GWI position to be lower than their pay – while the reverse is true for the other group – they are very low paid. Let us refer to the first group as 'artisan occupations' and the other group as 'routine professional occupations'.

What is interesting about these two clusters of occupations is that even though they are at polar opposites of the pay spectrum on average (the average percentile position of artisan occupations is only 25.5, while it is 78.6 for routine professional occupations), their relative GWI scores are more or less the same overall: routine professional occupations have an average GWI percentile position of 55.8, while for artisan occupations it is 56.3. How can two clusters of occupations at polar ends of the pay spectrum end up having relatively similar overall job quality?

Table 4.10 lists the GWI scores and dimension scores of both these two broad clusters of occupations. Overall, there is only a slight difference in GWI scores between the two clusters with artisan occupations being 0.073 GWI units worse than routine professional occupations – equivalent to one fifth of a standard deviation. As before, we can decompose why their GWIs are different. The main reason is the lower task variety in artisan occupations, but also important are less control over work time and lower chances for participation opportunities. Nonetheless, artisan occupations enjoy much better skill-use and have slightly higher task discretion than routine professional occupations, which offsets this. Both these factors weigh heavily in the GWI. Interestingly, artisan occupations have slightly better job security, and this also contributes to equalizing GWI scores between the two groups.

Finally, one advantage of being able to look at the occupational unit group level is that we can explore within-class inequalities more. While the class structure captures the broad contours of disparities in Good Work fairly well, looking at the occupational structure more directly at the unit group level of course does a more fine-grained job.

How durable are occupational quality disparities?

Whether one maps disparities in the quality of work by class or detailed occupation, stratification theory expects occupation is important however defined. Recall how in the Goldthorpe model of occupational class, each class category is supposed to represent a shared set of employment relations which in turn lead to enduring differences in economic life chances between classes. One potential criticism of this approach is that classes do not necessarily mean the

Table 4.10: Decomposing differences in GWI scores between 'artisan occupations' and 'routine professionals'

	'Artisan occupations'	'Routine professionals'	Difference	Explained (%)
GWI score	2.949	3.022	−0.073	
Log hourly pay score	0.004	0.006	−0.002	2.6
Job security score	0.727	0.719	0.008	−10.9
Continuous learning score	0.087	0.098	−0.011	15.7
Skill-use score	0.907	0.881	0.026	−35.6
Task variety score	0.545	0.600	−0.055	75.2
Task discretion score	0.526	0.515	0.011	−15.0
Job demands score	−0.066	−0.065	−0.001	1.3
Work time control score	0.052	0.082	−0.030	41.4
Participation opportunities score	0.167	0.185	−0.019	25.4

Notes: All workers aged 20 to 60 in the Skills and Employment Surveys 2006, 2012 and 2017.

same thing over time. That is, the economic life prospects attached to a class category might not be constant across time. Some elements of stratification research suggested a weakening of the class effect (sometimes called the 'death of class thesis'). A similar criticism might be extended to the quality of working life. Has the relationship between occupational position and job quality been weakening over

Figure 4.5: Explanatory power of occupation across Good Work dimensions over time

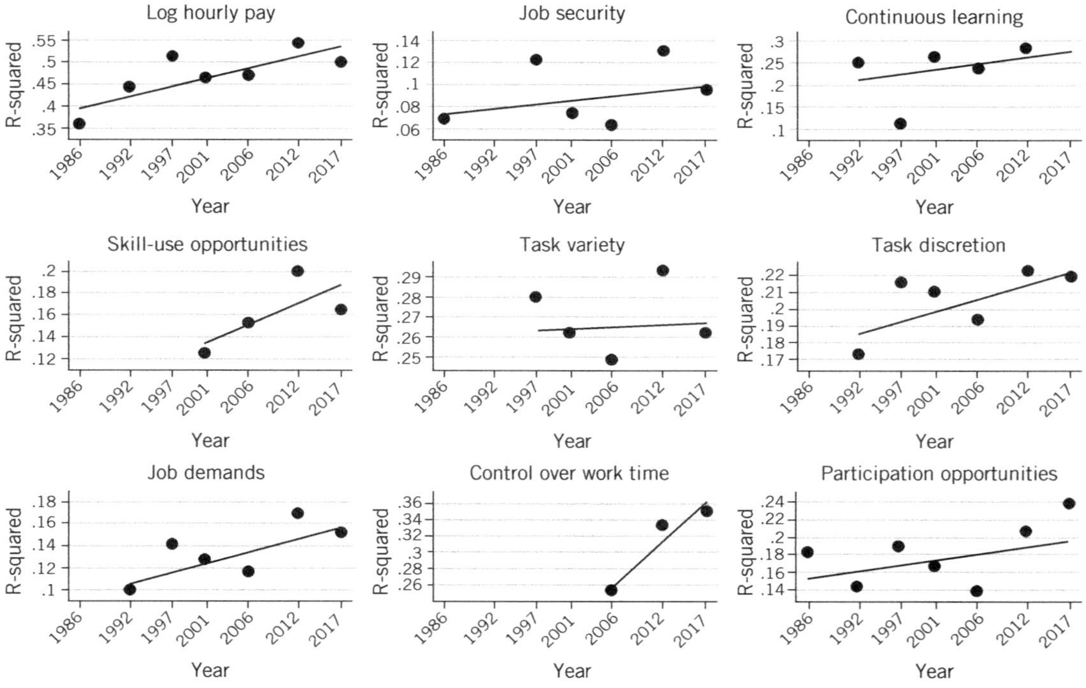

Notes: All workers aged 20 to 60 in the Skills and Employment Surveys 2006, 2012 and 2017.

time? Figure 4.5 explores this idea using the R-squared from separate OLS regressions for each job quality dimension by year (1986–2017), including all 205 detailed occupation unit groups as the only independent variables. Although most variation in Good Work dimensions is within occupations (except for pay in recent years), the figure shows it has generally been increasing. This means one's occupation is becoming a better predictor of not just pay as revealed in prior research, but also job quality more widely, validating that taking an occupational perspective is becoming more and not less relevant over time. Controlling for the changing composition of occupations using the standard set of controls in other analyses shows a similar trend (not shown). Additionally, Figure 4.6 repeats the same exercise for the GWI and for job satisfaction. It shows a generally similar trend of the increasing explanatory power of occupation. Thus, overall, one's occupation is becoming a better predictor of one's quality of working life as far back as we can observe each indicator in the SES over the last three decades. It is an open question why this might be the case and one we do not attempt to address here. For our purposes, it simply highlights that taking an occupational approach is becoming more valid over time as a way of understanding the quality of individuals' jobs.

A second criticism of an occupational approach to mapping Good Work is that there must be substantial variations within occupations. Clearly, a measure of Good Work at the job level is preferred to one at the occupation level. Despite the attractiveness of this argument, a practical limitation is that detailed information on job quality is often unavailable in national surveys. It is therefore useful to create an occupational proxy that can be used to impute information about the quality of work into datasets that contain information on occupation but not job quality. We can aggregate the job-level job quality scores to the occupation level and then take the mean GWI in each occupation as an indicator of the average job quality

Figure 4.6: Explanatory power of occupation for the GWI and job satisfaction over time

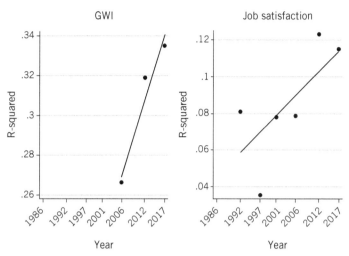

Notes: All workers aged 20 to 60 in the Skills and Employment Surveys 2006, 2012 and 2017.

Table 4.11: Comparison of the job-level indicators with occupation-level GWI

	Correlation
GWI score	0.470
Log hourly pay	0.673
Job security	0.138
Continuous learning	0.454
Skill-use	0.324
Task variety	0.467
Task discretion	0.392
Job demands	0.280
Work time control	0.501
Participation opportunities	0.334
Job satisfaction	0.203

Notes: All workers aged 20 to 60 in the Skills and Employment Surveys 2006, 2012 and 2017.

in the entire occupation. As can be seen in Table 4.11, the correlations between job-level and occupational-level GWI scores are reasonably strong. The same is the case for the Good Work dimensions. However, there is variation according to specific measure. For instance, the correlation is noticeably smaller for job security than for, say, pay. This might be because job security very much depends on the workplace or industry, and pay less so; it depends more on the going rates in occupational labour markets. Nonetheless, our findings echo those found in previous research examining the relationship between occupation and the quality of work, which concluded 'if you want to know whether a stranger has a relatively good or bad job the best single question you can ask him or her is still what he or she does for a living'.[15] These occupation-level scores will be used in later chapters when job-level information is not available.

Are the highest-quality occupations the most satisfying occupations?

Finally, having demonstrated that Good Work is stratified by the occupational structure in varied ways (and increasingly so), we move on to explore whether the highest quality occupations – those with the highest overall job quality as revealed by the GWI – really are the most satisfying ones. The results are reported in Figure 4.7. It shows that individuals in those occupations scoring higher in the GWI tend to report higher job satisfaction, but the correlation is quite modest. This modest correlation illustrates the point made in the previous chapter that Good Work is distinct from job satisfaction. There are many determinants of job satisfaction other than job quality, hence our argument that the GWI is a proxy for the satisfaction *potential* of an occupation given observed job features. Nonetheless, exploring how other factors might moderate occupationally differentiated job

Figure 4.7: Mean GWI and mean overall job satisfaction across occupations

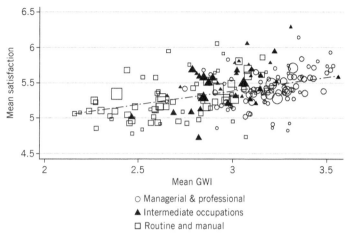

Notes: All workers aged 20 to 60 in the Skills and Employment Surveys 2006, 2012 and 2017.

quality is critically important, an issue we turn to in the next chapter.

Summary and conclusions

• In general, the more an occupation pays, the better its overall job quality. The occupational quality structure broadly corresponds to the occupational class structure.

• However, there are many interesting exceptions to this. For instance, we identify a group of 'artisan occupations' that are some of the lowest paid but have modest overall job quality (such as beauticians, clergy, hairdressers, pub landlords and bakers).

• Conversely, we also identify a group of 'routine professionals' that are some of the highest paid but have only modest overall job quality (mainly related to finance, law, IT and various other licensed professions). Class captures disparities quite well, but the class hierarchy is not the same as the Good Work hierarchy. Within the intermediate class, small employers and own-account workers stand out as having job quality comparable to managerial and professional workers.

- Occupations are becoming a better predictor of all job-quality dimensions as far back as we can observe each indicator in the SES.
- Individuals in occupations with higher GWI scores are generally more satisfied than those with low GWI scores, but the correlation is modest, justifying the view that job quality cannot be equated with job satisfaction.

FIVE

The Changing Occupational Quality Structure

Introduction

This final empirical chapter explores what has been happening to the occupational structure from a Good Work perspective, and what is likely to happen to it in the near future. First, it outlines some of the main theoretical perspectives informing our expectations about the evolution in the occupational structure and then portrays the actual trends using the SESs 1986 to 2017. Second, it explores what the future may hold for the continued evolution of the occupational structure by exploring the relationship between automation probability and occupational quality. Finally, it explores the changes in job quality within occupations by occupational quality quintiles.

Technology and the changing structure of the labour market

Debates over the role of technology in transforming the occupational structure are not new. However, there has been a reinvigoration in the issue in recent years following the publication of an influential study by University of Oxford–based engineers Carl Frey and Michael Osborne, which boldly proclaimed that 47 per cent of employment in the United States could be fully automated by the year 2033.[1] This prompted a series of studies exploring the issue, including a UK-specific one using the same methodology putting the figure at 35 per cent.[2] Nonetheless, employment in the UK is at record levels, as it is across many other countries at a similar stage of economic development. Even after four industrial revolutions, these sorts of doomsday scenarios of work disappearing for good have never come to fruition, largely because they suffer from the 'lump of labour fallacy'. That is, it ignores the fact that while some occupations may decline, others emerge and grow. In other words, the overall employment rate is not fixed.

There is, however, also a related and much more legitimate anxiety that technology not only affects the quantity of work in aggregate, but also its overall quality through changing the occupational mix and changing the relative quality of individual occupations. Three broad perspectives can be identified from far older literatures that the more contemporary debates have effectively reinvigorated. They all share one thing in common and that is the major role of technology in transforming the occupational structure. The main way each perspective differs is in the implications of technological development for the overall quality of work. We can identify an optimistic perspective, a pessimistic one and a third that can be described as the polarization perspective. Each one is briefly outlined.

The *optimistic perspective* postulates that technological development implies steadily more complex and varied types of occupations that require higher levels of skills. This is because machines can increasingly replace the tasks in routine and manual occupations, which frees up labour to work in more non–routine and non–manual occupations that require the mastery of specialist knowledge such as teachers, scientists and doctors. These sorts of occupations also become increasingly productive due to technological change and so the demand for labour in this type of occupation increases. This perspective is encapsulated in a body of research carried out in the 1960s and 1970s, examples of which include Robert Blauner's 1964 *Alienation and Freedom: The Factory Worker and His Industry* and Daniel Bell's 1974 *The Coming of Post-Industrial Society*, the latter of which popularized the notion of 'knowledge work'. In economics, empirical work has labelled this general upgrading of the occupational structure as 'skill-biased technical change'. This reformulation of the 'post-industrial society' thesis states that technological change tends to be biased in favour of skilled work. An additional insight from this strand of research is that it acknowledges the supply side to the story: the growth in graduates ('skilled' workers) that are said to be better placed to take advantage of the growth in 'skilled' occupations relative to non-graduates ('unskilled' workers) is another complementary reason for the upgrading of the occupational structure in addition to shifts in demand. All strands point to a rosy picture of a general upgrading of the occupational structure through an expansion of higher-quality occupations at the expense of lower-quality ones.

Against this, there is the *pessimistic perspective*. While this perspective acknowledges that technology induces a decline in generally poorer-quality routine and manual occupations and a rise in generally higher-quality non–routine and non-manual occupations, it states that technology aids the routinization and deskilling of all classes of occupation. In other words, it highlights another mechanism via which technology can shape the occupational quality structure other than changing the occupational mix – through deteriorating the quality of work *within* occupations. These accounts unsurprisingly tend to have a Marxian flavour to them. Classic texts in this tradition were Harry Braverman's *Labour and Monopoly Capital: The Degradation of Work in the Twentieth Century* (1974), published in the same year as Bell's classic. This spoke of the deskilling of craft occupations – occupations traditionally having a great deal of discretion and skill-use – aided by development of the production line and associated technology. Technology helps capital to widen and strengthen its grip over the labour process in various ways, for instance through tighter monitoring, fragmentation of tasks and increasing managerial control. Developments in technology, this perspective argues, increasingly allows managers to practise scientific management par excellence. Richard Edwards' *Contested Terrain: The Transformation of the Workplace in the Twentieth Century*, published in 1979, more or less extended this notion to include professional work, where technology aids the growth in centralized bureaucratic control systems within organizations. More recent examples include George Ritzer's *McDonaldization of Society*, coming in 1993. It argued the control strategies practised in low-wage fast-food occupations were percolating upwards through the occupational structure into middle-skill and professional work. In short, the pessimistic accounts argue that even with an expansion of knowledge work and an increasing number of graduates to fill these new positions, technology allows capital to extract an ever-increasing share of surplus value from workers through degrading all categories of occupations. Aggregate trends in the falling share of income going to labour – optimized in Thomas Piketty's tome *Capital in the Twenty-First Century* published in 2013 – broadly support the increasing extraction of surplus value part. However, more direct, systematic and representative evidence for this perspective regarding actual work tasks beyond small-scale workplace case studies is hard to come by.

The third perspective, the *polarization perspective*, by contrast, states that technology implies both positive and negative trends in that there is a simultaneous growth in high-paid *and* low-paid occupations, with a decline in middle-paid ones. One earlier influential account in this regard was Robert Reich's *The Work of Nations*, published in 1991. Reich suggested the occupational structure can be divided into three broad groups: symbolic analysts, routine production and in-person service workers. In contrast to the optimistic perceptive, which predicts a growth in the first category of occupations and a decline in the second type, the polarization thesis also predicts a growth in the third type of lower-paid and lower-quality work as well, resulting in a polarizing occupational structure. Most of the applied work on the polarization thesis comes from economists. Economist David Autor has been at the centre of this research in the United States. They argue technological change is 'task-biased' as it is good at substituting tasks in routine occupations but not non-routine ones. This leads to a decline in not only routine manual occupations (often found in manufacturing) but also routine non-manual occupations (such as clerical and back-office occupations). On the other hand, technology complements non-routine tasks, which leads to a growth in non-routine manual and non-manual occupations. Unlike the optimistic perspective, the polarization thesis states that the growing occupations include not only high-paying knowledge occupations, but also low-paid non-routine manual occupations such as care assistants, taxi drivers, couriers and bar staff (which Reich calls in-person services). In sum, the polarization perspective posits a simultaneous growth in both low-quality *and* high-quality occupations, and a decline in middle-quality ones.

Collectively, these three perspectives connect the occupational structure to aggregate changes in the quality of work through two main mechanisms. The first is through changes in the occupational mix, that is, differential growth rates across occupations. Some occupations grow and some decline while others remain constant. The second mechanism connecting the occupational structure to the quality of work is through the changing quality of work attached to each occupational position themselves. In other words, even if the occupational mix remained unchanged, technology may have altered the quality of work attached to those positions. This second mechanism is the main proposition of the pessimistic perspective, while the optimistic and polarization thesis are mainly about shifts in the occupational structure.

A great deal of empirical work now exists on this first mechanism. It strongly supports the polarization thesis across countries.[3] In the British context, an influential paper published by Maarten Goos and Alan Manning in 2007,[4] found there had been a decline in middle-paying occupations, a large growth in high-paying occupations and a smaller but significant growth in low-paid occupations from 1979 to 1999. It was a UK version of an earlier analysis of the evolution in the occupational structure of the United States by Erick Ohlin Wright and Rachel Dwyer.[5] The polarization perspective has been very influential in UK policy circles, with the then Department of Business, Innovation and Skills publishing a paper on the issue.[6]

A limitation of this strand of research is that it assumes stability in the occupational pay structure. Research shows growing differences between occupations are becoming increasingly important in explaining general growing wage inequality.[7] While we can learn a great deal from charting stability and change in the opportunity structure through shifts in the occupational structure, even if the rank ordering of the opportunities attached to positions is constant the qualities attached to them may have changed. For instance, one of the authors of this book has shown, in various ways, that historical trends in growing wage inequality, and more recent trends in zero-hours contracts and pay-for-performance, have all been class-biased. A second issue is the narrow definition of job quality adopted in these studies. With a few exceptions, few studies have explored whether the labour market has polarized in terms of the overall quality of work measured beyond pay.[8] It remains largely unknown whether the pattern of polarization can be extended to a fuller multidimensional definition of job quality. The next two sections explore changes in the occupational quality structure in terms of both the occupational mix and the quality of work attached to occupational positions.

Trends in the occupational quality structure

The first way the occupational structure relates to changes to the quality of work is through changes in the occupational mix: the growth and decline in employment across occupational quality categories. One criticism of the very influential polarization thesis and associated evidence for the Good Work agenda is that it explored growth rates in employment across occupational categories defined in terms of pay. To explore what has been happening to the occupational employment structure in terms of occupational quality, we classify occupations into roughly equally sized quintiles based on their mean GWI scores and employment in 2012/17. Classifying occupations in this way is the main analytical approach in this literature, so we adopt it here for comparison. We pool adjacent SES years to increase the number of observations within each occupation cell. Repeating the analysis without pooling years and defining occupations at a higher level of aggregation of 81 occupations (three-digit) instead of our 200+ occupations (based on a recode of the four-digit codes to give sufficient sample sizes) as an alternative to increase occupational N results in qualitatively similar findings.[9]

Figure 5.1 explores changes in the occupational structure by classifying occupations into quintiles according to mean pay and mean GWI scores. The panel on the right shows a general decline in low- to moderate-quality occupations, and a rise in higher-quality occupations. This is in stark contrast to the occupational pay perspective (the panel on the left), where we can broadly replicate the pattern of polarization revealed by previous research using different data. The percentage change in employment within occupational quintiles is further broken down by subperiod. We find that most of the decline in middle-paying occupations and growth in higher-paying occupations occurred in the 1980s and 1990s, while the growth in lower-paying occupations is a more recent phenomenon. This implies that technological change upgraded the occupational structure

Figure 5.1: The changing occupational structure 1986/92 to 2012/17

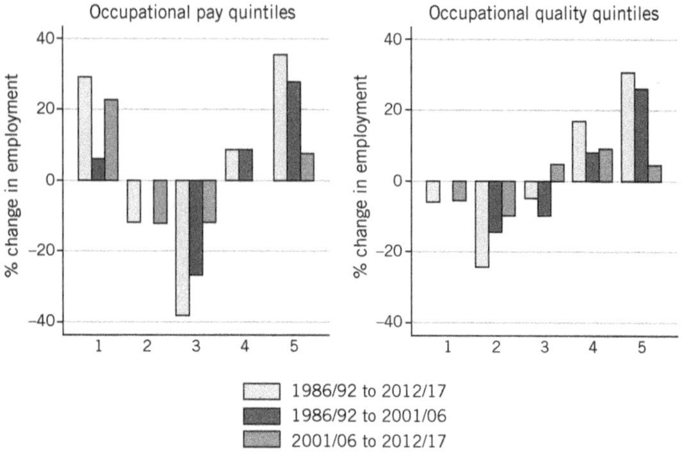

Occupational pay quintiles   Occupational quality quintiles

1986/92 to 2012/17
1986/92 to 2001/06
2001/06 to 2012/17

Notes: All workers aged 20 to 60 in the Skills and Employment Surveys 1986, 1992, 2001, 2006, 2012 and 2017.

by replacing middle-paying manufacturing and clerical jobs with managerial and professional ones. The fact the growth in lower-paying occupations is more recent supports the view that their growth was not only driven by technological change affecting labour demand but also by shifts in the supply of workers willing and able to do these jobs – such as the influx of Eastern European workers following the enlargement of the European Union in the early 2000s. Similar results were also found in other research that is critical of technology being responsible for the (wage) polarization of the labour market.[10]

If we rank occupations by their overall quality (their average GWI scores) and map employment change across occupational quality quintiles, a different picture emerges. We find a general decline in the three lowest occupational quality quintiles and a general and much larger proportionate rise in the highest two occupational quality quintiles. Patterns between subperiods are a bit more complex, but the general overall pattern since the mid-1980s is one of general occupational upgrading. This is in stark contrast to the polarization thesis, which has become a powerful narrative in recent years – and has often been extended to debates about the quality of work defined more broadly than pay. If we define occupational quality multidimensionally to include features of work related to development and fulfilment à la Taylor Review (DBEIS, 2017), we find a much rosier picture of historical shifts in the occupational structure. While this may seem consistent with the optimistic perspective, it must be noted that the growth in the highest quintiles has slowed somewhat in the most recent period.

Given that the GWI is a summary index, it is necessary to construct occupational quality hierarchies in other ways. We can rank occupations according to their scores on each of the other eight indicators (other than pay) and trace out how these different dimensions of occupational quality have evolved. If all these different ways of defining occupational quality hierarchies point to upgrading, then we can be more confident that shifts in the occupational structure can be best characterized as one of general upgrading as opposed to polarization. These analyses are reported in Figure 5.2. We find clear occupational upgrading (declines in the lowest quintiles, rises in the highest quintiles) when occupational quality is defined in terms of learning, skill-use, task variety, work time control and participation. We also find occupational 'upgrading' in the case of job demands, but that there has been a growth in occupations with higher job demands might not strictly be defined as 'upgrading' since higher job demands potentially lower employee well-being.

For occupational task discretion, while we find a substantial growth in occupations with the highest average levels of task discretion and a decline in those with the lowest levels, we do find a small growth in occupations in the second quintile. This might be summarized as 'weak occupational upgrading' with respect to this aspect of occupational quality. The occupational quality hierarchy where we find evidence

Figure 5.2: The changing occupational quality structure according to alternative definitions 1986/92 to 2012/17

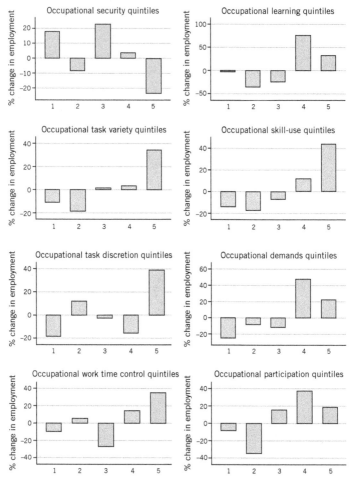

Notes: All workers aged 20 to 60 in the Skills and Employment Surveys 1986, 1992, 2001, 2006, 2012 and 2017.

of what might be termed occupational downgrading is with respect to the occupational-security hierarchy. Here, we find a simultaneous growth in the lowest quintiles and decline in the highest quintiles, indicating that jobs have been declining in the most secure occupations but growing in the least secure. Nonetheless, the picture is not one of wholescale occupational downgrading as we also find growth in jobs in occupations with moderate, average security. Part of the reason why the findings for the occupational-security hierarchy stand out as quite ambiguous might be that job security is the Good Work indicator that is least related to occupational position, as was shown in Figure 4.5. Notwithstanding the exceptions of job demands and job security, taking all these indicators together, we find a picture of general occupational upgrading across the occupational quality structure.

One final way to reinterpret what has been happening to the occupational structure is to explore the fraction of employment in different occupational classes (Figure 5.3).[11] By this measure, too, we find one of general occupational upgrading. There was a clear expansion in the managerial and professional occupations and a clear fall in routine and manual occupations. In 1986, 45 per cent of the labour force were employed in semi-routine and routine occupations. By 2017, 45 per cent of the labour force were employed in managerial and professional occupations. There is also a slight decline in the middle of the class structure. When defining occupational quality in terms of NS-SEC categories, again, we find no evidence of polarization, but rather one of general upgrading.

Automation and the occupational quality structure

The evidence thus far has presented a rather rosy picture of how the occupational structure has evolved since the mid-1980s when the occupational hierarchy is defined to include broader features of work related to development and fulfilment. A natural next question is whether technology is likely continue to

Figure 5.3: The changing class structure 1986/92 to 2012/17

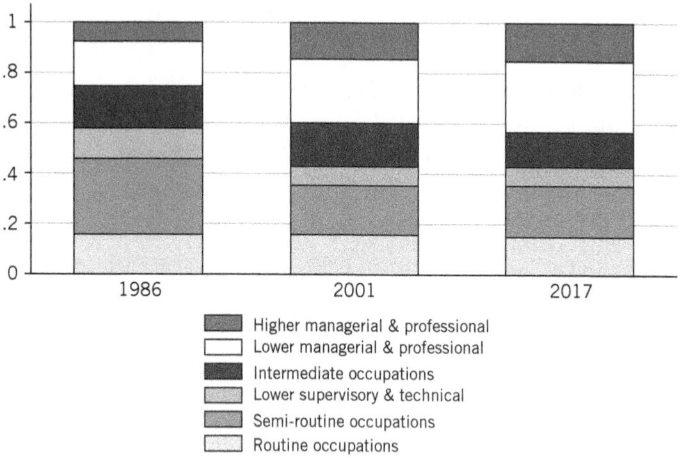

Higher managerial & professional
Lower managerial & professional
Intermediate occupations
Lower supervisory & technical
Semi-routine occupations
Routine occupations

Notes: All workers aged 20 to 60 in the Skills and Employment Surveys 1986, 2001 and 2017.

have a generally benign effect on the occupational structure. Of course, there is no way to know for sure. However, amid all the anxiety surrounding automation, there is now a variety of automation potential and automation probability scores floating around. Researchers tend to calculate these scores at the occupational level. We can therefore take these indicators (if you believe them) and map them against measures of occupational quality. Such an exercise is reported in Figure 5.4 using the ONS automation potential scores.[12] Whether we defined the occupational quality structure in terms of pay or the GWI, we find that it is the lowest-paid and lowest overall quality occupations that have the highest automation potential, whereas the highest-paid and highest-quality occupations have the lowest automation potential. Overall, although it is hard to predict the future,[13] this figure demonstrates that the occupational quality structure is likely to continue to evolve in favourable ways. Whether displaced workers will end up benefiting from these trends by transitioning to higher-quality occupations, though, is another question entirely.

Figure 5.4: Automation potential across occupations

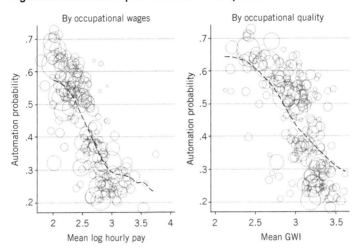

Notes: All workers aged 20 to 60 in the Skills and Employment Surveys 2006, 2012 and 2017. Automation potential scores obtained from ONS (2019b).

Trends in the nature of the occupational quality structure

While exploring how technology relates to the occupational structure both in the recent past and possibly the recent future finds a generally optimistic picture (with some important exceptions regarding job security and job demands), recall how the pessimistic perspective is about the quality of work *within* occupations changes over time. While it is well known that there is broad stability in occupational rankings in terms of pay (and the other Good Work dimensions), the average distance between occupations in these indicators might be growing or declining. In other words, the highest-quality occupations might be getting even better, while the lowest-quality occupations might be getting even worse.

To investigate this issue, Figure 5.5 reports average job quality by survey year and occupational quality quintile. Note here that

Figure 5.5: Job quality trends by occupational quality quintile

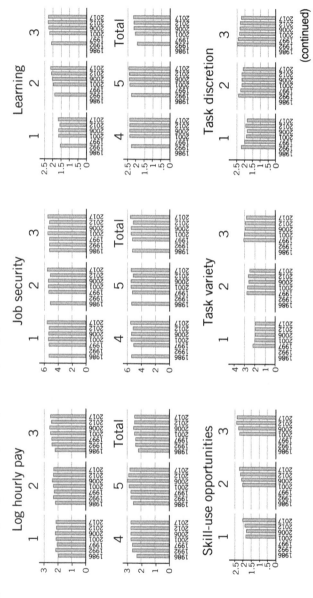

(continued)

Figure 5.5: Job quality trends by occupational quality quintile (continued)

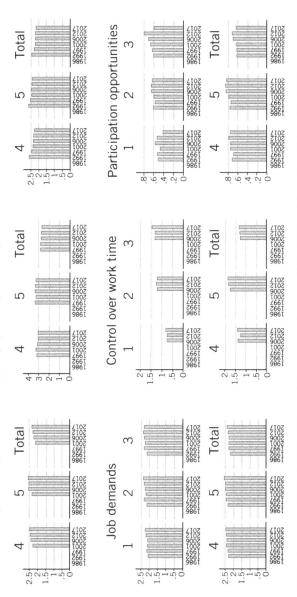

Notes: All workers aged 20 to 60 in the Skills and Employment Surveys 1986, 1992, 2001, 2006, 2012 and 2017. X-axes refer to survey year and y-axes refer to the mean scores of the specific job quality indicator (see Table 3.1 for question wording and coding scheme of each). Graphs drawn by occupational quality quintile.

given not all indicators were asked in all survey years: some only go back to 2006, while others go back further. Only pay and job security were measured in 1986 (the furthest back we can go in the SES). Two main findings emerge from this analysis. The first is that across all these separate dimensions, the occupational hierarchy holds in each one such that the higher occupational quality quintiles scores highest across all indicators and the lower-occupational quality quintiles score lowest across all indicators. In other words, the overall occupational quality hierarchy holds across all indicators. The second finding is that, with the possible exception of pay, trends within occupational quality quintiles are broadly similar across different indicators of occupational quality. In other words, there appears to be little evidence of growing divergence across the GWI indicators between occupational quality quintiles. If an indicator is found to be rising or falling, it is doing so within each occupational quality quintile, if by differing rates. In short, what is happening in each occupational quality quintile is broadly reflective of overall trends in job quality – which are indicated in the panels marked 'Total'.

Even though the trends in occupational quality structure can be characterized as one of general upgrading, supporting the optimistic perspective, the qualities attached to occupational positions has been changing. Some of these trends are favour-able: there has been a general rise in pay (although this has stagnated since 2012), continuous learning requirements, skill-use opportunities and participation opportunities – with a flatter though not negative trend in job security. On the flipside, there have also been some broadly negative trends: there has been a general decline in task variety and task discretion, as well as a rise in job demands, as the pessimistic perspective might have predicted. While the rise in job demands might be expected given a general rise in the fraction of jobs in more demanding occupations, there was a precipitous decline in task variety and task discretion within all occupational quality quintiles – although it was most severe for the lowest occupational quality quintile. In other words, while the occupational opportunity structure for more fulfilling working lives generally shifted in a favourable way, this transformation did not necessarily translate into better job quality with respect to specifically task variety, task discretion and job demands. This is a somewhat alarming finding (and one which has been known within the academic literature for some time[14]) as it potentially has big implications for the Good Work agenda, where the quality of work is defined in terms of more than just pay and security, to include the potential of work to be fulfilling. As Chapter Two made clear, task variety and task discretion are the second- and fourth-most important factors respectively for determining job satisfaction. While job demands on its own was only weakly associated with job satisfaction, other research shows it interacts with control over work and being in high-pressured low-control work can negatively affect health.[15]

While the occupational quality structure quite clearly has upgraded as the optimistic perspective has predicted, supporting the pessimistic perspective, we find that some of this has been offset by declining task variety and task discretion, coupled with growing job demands. While we find the quality of work is occupationally differentiated, work is getting more routine, more controlled and more intense for workers in all occupations. We therefore suggest that the evidence presented here in fact represents a fourth perspective what might be termed the 'nuanced upgrading' perspective. While the occupational structure has generally been upgrading, some of this positive trend has been offset by declining job quality in three critical dimensions within all occupational quality quintiles: task variety, task discretion and job demands. What this implies for the Good Work agenda will be discussed in more details in the next chapter.

Summary and conclusions

• When defining the occupational quality structure in terms of overall job quality, there is little evidence the labour market has polarized since the mid-1980s. In general, the occupational quality structure has been upgrading through an expansion in the highest-quality occupations and decline in lower-quality occupations. However, the pace of upgrading has stalled since the 2000s.

- In general, the lowest-quality occupations are most at risk of automation, with the highest-quality occupations having the lowest risk, implying a potentially positive evolution in the occupational structure with respect to overall job quality.

- However, job quality has been getting worse in three critical respects across the occupational spectrum. Work has been getting more routine, more controlled and more intense for all workers.

- Depending on the extent to which displaced workers can smoothly transition into growing higher-quality occupations, a potentially more urgent issue is the declining intrinsic job quality of all workers.

SIX

Conclusions and Implications

This book attempted to address the following questions:

1. What makes work good?
2. What is the structure of occupational quality?
3. What has been happening to the occupational quality structure?
4. What are the policy implications of the answers to questions 1 to 3?

Our answers to the first three are as follows. Good Work is rich in intrinsic rewards, which, according to workers themselves, are powerful in shaping their well-being. The quality of work is highly uneven across the occupational structure and these inequalities are not only enduring but also becoming more entrenched. This implies that one's occupation – one's broad field of work – structures who can achieve the highest levels of job-related well-being, and increasingly so. Bad Work (which tends to be routine) is increasingly being replaced by technology, while Good Work (which tends to non-routine) is growing and set to grow further. Moreover, the higher the quality of an occupation, the lower the probability it is likely to automatable. This means that the future of Good Work is potentially rather rosy.

Along the way, there are many nuances, that might seem counter-intuitive at first glance, to these broad findings. Some provide a somewhat optimistic picture, others a more worrying one. Starting with the optimistic ones, Chapter Three showed that Good Work does not necessarily mean high-paying work. There are many lower- or moderate-paying occupations that score very highly on the critical intrinsic aspects of work, and so score highly on the GWI that this book introduces and advocates as a way of monitoring national progress on it. The identification of these exceptional occupations such as beauticians, hairdressers, publicans and bakers should give hope to those who do not aspire to work in managerial and professional occupations as these jobs are not the only route to 'Good Work'. Conversely, there are many high-paying occupations with decent security, which we term 'routine professionals' – occupations related to finance, law and information technology – that score relatively poorly on these intrinsic dimensions, and so are characterized by much lower scores on the GWI than their pay alone would suggest. Overall, then, both categories score relatively similarly. Findings such as these should be informative to those occupying the latter category that winning further pay rises might not bring much additional happiness, while moving to a line of work that allows more scope for fulfilment might be a better solution in achieving the Good Work ideal.

At the same time, this book highlights the fact that a large fraction of the labour force are employed in very poor-quality work. There are few surprises in which occupations are at the bottom end of the Good Work hierarchy – low-paying service occupations such cleaners, call-centre workers, check-out operators and waiters. On the one hand, Chapter Five found that this sort of work is in decline as technology continues to replace them – which should be good news for realizing the Good Work ideal – provided those exiting this sort of work escape it to higher-quality occupational categories. On the other, it reinforces the need for mobility policies to enable those in disappearing forms of work (of whatever quality) to not only transition to another line of work, but to something better. This book provides the previously missing multidimensional yardstick to judge whether another type of work is in fact 'better' overall. This should provide more effective and better targeted interventions. It implies some workers in careers with less scope for fulfilment may need to change careers if they are to improve their quality of working life, reinforcing the need for governmental help (for instance in terms of retraining) around mobility and progression up the Good Work hierarchy.

While this book provides some further grounds for optimism as the occupational quality structure has been changing in generally favourable ways, there have, however, been some worrying trends where there can be no positive spin, and urgent collective attention is required. Even in highest-quality occupations, things have been getting worse or not improving along certain critical intrinsic dimensions. While technology has led to positive developments in occupational structure, it has undoubtedly stifled many of the enjoyable aspects of work, even in those occupational positions where the chances of them are highest. It was found that work for all occupational categories is becoming more routine, more controlled and more intense. Mostly likely, changes in technology are partly responsible for these trends. These findings about the changing quality of occupations highlights that while upward mobility can improve the quality of working life for those in low-quality occupations, it is not a panacea on its own for increasing the quality of work overall.

Implications for mapping Good Work

So, what are the implications of our findings? Current employment policies tend to place a greater emphasis on extrinsic aspects of work – such as pay, hours, security, breaks and holidays – and ensuring they are properly enforced. This book shows that the Good Work agenda could go further.

While policies that make work fair and decent win widespread support, can policies that increase the potential of work to offer development and fulfilment attain the same level support? Our answer to this question is that if we want to improve the quality of work, defined multidimensionally, we need to make it more visible. If we want to improve the quality of work for all, we need to map and publicize it. A better-informed public can make better career decisions. We have several recommendations in this regard.

We believe there is scope for a *national index of job quality along the lines of GWI.*[1] The one we have developed here is essentially like a measure of inflation, but the basket of goods is job features and the weights are how the factors affect overall job satisfaction. The weights can therefore vary each year – or perhaps each decade, given the slow pace of change – to keep up to date with what workers value. This also implies the ingredients to defining Good Work may potentially shift over time – much like how the basket of goods that constitutes the calculation of inflation changes to reflect spending habits. While summary indices can obscure more than they reveal, an attractive feature of the GWI is that it can identify why overall job quality is changing. Changes in the GWI can be decomposed into components reflecting changes in worker expectations as well as changes in underlying job quality. This can pinpoint why overall job quality is increasing or decreasing: is it due to changes in expectations or changes in the underlying quantities? We argue that the main attraction of a single index, however, lies in its ability to rank occupations (or indeed other groups such as workplaces, cities, regions and so forth) along a meaningful metric to map enduring disparities. A related attractive feature is that we can also decompose differences between groups, so gaps between social groups (such as classes or genders) can not only be mapped, but explained. Relying simply on measures of job satisfaction to chart changes as an overall measure would miss out on any explanation for those trends, while our index can explain differences with reference to its theoretically meaningful ingredients.

Relatedly, we contend the Good Work agenda *should be well-being centred but well-being itself is not job quality*. Job satisfaction cannot be a measure of job quality per se as it is not a feature of the job. It depends on many other things, many of which are not connected to the job at all (expectations, social comparisons, personal quirks and so on). At the time of writing, it appears the government has included measures of well-being as one of its national indicators of job quality.[2] Focusing on satisfaction with one's job as an intrinsic feature of it rather than a subjective evaluation of it inhibits the proper identification of the structure of enduring disparities in the quality of working lives in the population. Nonetheless, reports of job satisfaction are useful for constructing an overall index as they inform us how important different job qualities, and only those qualities, are for workers in terms of their well-being for the population rather than specific individuals.

Finally, *any Good Work strategy should also map disparities by class and occupation*. The mapping of Good Work should not just focus on year-to-year changes in national progress, but also the closing or widening of existing and enduring inequalities between occupational groups. The most critical element of the book's argument is that while monitoring trends in the quality of work is an essential step in improving it, disparities should be a key aspect of its mapping. Given that more intrinsic features of work are often considered less tractable than, say, differences in pay, this can make disparities in them less visible. Moreover, occupations are a useful unit of analysis for making disparities transparent. When we normally think of disparities at work, we might usually think of social categories such as gender, ethnicity, disability and so on. This book argues that occupation is as important, if not more so, in the context of the quality of work. This is because it is likely that much of the existing disparity between social groups, as conventionally defined, is attributable to occupational segregation between social groups (that is, different social groups end up doing different types of work). Given there are disparities in the quality of work life chances across occupations and that mobility across occupations is low, the final argument is that occupations provide a sound basis by which to map enduring disparities. This could be extended to the mapping of topical features of 'Bad Work' too. As an example, zero-hour contracts are incredibly concentrated. Recent evidence finds that over half are in just ten occupations.[3] Findings such as these highlight the concentrated nature of certain aspects of job quality and a better understanding of the dispersion and concentration of labour-market phenomena can lead to more effective policy interventions and targeted action by unions. Publishing national statistics on detailed dimensions of the quality of work by detailed occupation would be a tremendously useful resource.

Another practical advantage of an occupational approach is that the occupational classifications are common across data sources and are in fact widely used already in policy and social surveys and in administrative data: for example, in identifying shortage occupations for immigration policy. By focusing on occupations, we can map the quality of work back into historical datasets that did not directly measure it, if with somewhat less precision. Yet another advantage of focusing on occupations is that it means job quality information does not have to be collected in every survey or every year. The classification of occupational quality might be refreshed every decade or so through the remeasurement of the Good Work indicators – much like how the NS-SEC is rebased every decade for each new census – to economize on the costs of measurement.

From 'Good Work' to 'Good Careers'?

One's broad field of work, or occupation, is central to what we term the quality of work life chances, and increasingly so. Here, a distinction is made between job quality and the quality of working life. Whereas job quality refers to the quality of a job occupied by a given individual at any point in time, one's occupation is more of fixed constant in one's working life. It is therefore a convenient unit for mapping broader and more enduring disparities. To get a handle on enduring features of the quality of work, this book argues for an occupational perspective. That is, just as jobs vary in their core qualities, so do occupations. Occupations are clusters of functionally similar jobs. Given that mobility across occupations is relatively low, by simply knowing the qualities of work attached to specific occupations we have a reliable indicator of a given individual's experience of work over his or her entire working life (or at least a good chunk of it).

With our emphasis on occupational differentiation in the quality of work life chances, an obvious implication is that *occupational mobility is an underexplored route of improving the quality of working life*. But how realistic might this be? Our preliminary longitudinal research, which observes workers' career trajectories over two decades of their working lives has shown that upward occupational mobility leads to higher levels of job satisfaction, while downward mobility leads to dissatisfaction that lasts for many years after the transition.[4] This implies that there really is an occupational quality hierarchy. Moreover, it demonstrates that career changes do work, and that the *direction* of change is what really matters. Our other research shows that changing one's occupation has greater impact on subsequent well-being trajectories than changing employers.[5] This further implies that the quality of work life chances is stratified by occupation more than by the workplace. The government can support this with a lifelong education or retraining service, especially given that accelerating automation is destroying routine jobs.

Mobility and job-growth strategies should give more attention to occupation besides employers, industries and sectors. Policy related to employers is about workplaces, while industries are about product markets, but not what people are actually doing on a day-to-day basis, and this needs to change. Workplace policies are helpful in combating the poorest job quality within occupations. Our findings in Chapter Four revealed that the differences in job quality between the best and the worst jobs were greatest within occupational classes at the bottom of the labour market, whereas in managerial and professional occupations, job quality was less varied. This implies that workplaces have a greater role to play at the lower end than the top end. While workplace policies may be important, in aiming higher for the Good Work ideal, we also need to address the structural cracks and reduce the prevalence of poor-quality work in the first place. A potential approach is to complement the enforcement of minimum standards regulations regarding more extrinsic aspects of work with mobility policies to facilitate workers to transition to inherently more fulfilling work which, as this book reveals, is not always managerial and professional work.

Notes

Introduction

[1] There are various terms used in debates such as the quality of work, job quality, quality of working life, working conditions, Good Work and so on. We use these terms interchangeably. However, we recognize each specific term has their own academic origins and technical definitions depending on which source you read. Some of these definitional issues are reviewed later in the next chapter, but a full review is beyond the scope of this short empirically focused monograph when comprehensive summaries exist elsewhere (for instance, CIPD, 2017, 2018).

[2] DBEIS (2017: 6, emphasis added).

[3] HM Government (2018).

[4] Eurofound (2002); Cazes et al (2015).

[5] Regional governments and associations, as might be expected, have long had their own strategies, many of which have made substantial progress. Examples include the Welsh Fair Work Commission and the Scottish Fair Work Convention.

[6] DBEIS (2017). Also see the government's response (HM Government, 2018).

[7] The UK government has placed increased emphasis on employee well-being as a central policy goal, for instance with the setting up of the What Works for Wellbeing Centre in 2015, which, among other things, aims to connect government departments in terms of their role in shaping national well-being and to feed the latest evidence into practice (see https://whatworkswellbeing.org).

[8] Carnegie (2018).

[9] For instance, the ONS's first job quality publication was on pay, hours and contracts and adopted a 'threshold' approach to these issues (ONS, 2019a).

[10] The Carnegie Trust is once again taking a lead on this latter issue (Carnegie, 2020).

[11] For an easy-to-read introduction, see CIPD (2017). For an international review, see Burchell et al (2014).

[12] Grote and Guest (2017).

[13] Goldthorpe (2007).

[14] For a recent overview of the labour market segmentation approach, see Grimshaw et al (2017).

[15] See Williams (2013) for trends 1970s to 2000s and Williams (2017a) for the 2000s to 2010s.

[16] ONS (2017).

[17] Goos and Manning (2007).

Chapter One

[1] For instance, see the reports by the CIPD (CIPD, 2017, 2018b).

[2] For instance, see Clark and Georgellis (2013).

[3] See Zhou et al (2019).

[4] Nickell (1982); Goos and Manning (2007).

[5] Doeringer and Piore (1985); Grimshaw et al (2017).

[6] Braverman (1974); Goldthorpe and McKnight (2006); Gallie (2007); Kalleberg (2011).

[7] Hackman and Oldham (1980); Warr (1987); Karasek and Theorell (1990).

[8] Muñoz de Bustillo et al (2011); Felstead et al (2015).

[9] CIPD (2019).

[10] ONS (2019a).

[11] ONS (2019a).

[12] NRC (2010).

[13] For instance, see the classic Hawthorne studies that gave rise to the term the 'Hawthorne effect', popularized by Elton Mayo, often cited as the founder of the Human Relations movement, in *The Human Problems of an Industrialized Civilization* published in the 1930s.

[14] According to some academic commentaries, the proliferation and fragmentation of concepts and scales has severely limited the potential for impact of organizational psychology on workers, managers and, especially, policy (Grote and Guest, 2017).

[15] Goldthorpe (2016).

[16] Source: https://gtr.ukri.org/projects?ref=ES%2FP005292%2F1

[17] CIPD (2017); Carnegie (2018).

[18] See Felstead et al (2014) for more information on the SES methodology.

[19] Carnegie (2018).

[20] Lambert and Bihagen (2014).

[21] They are reviewed quite comprehensively in Muñoz de Bustillo et al (2011) who also develop a useful index, but with the weakness that the weights are decided by the researchers rather than workers themselves.

[22] For instance, Felstead et al (2019).

[23] Felstead et al (2019).

[24] Carnegie (2018).

[25] CIPD (2019).

[26] ONS (2019a).

Chapter Two

[1] The SES also asked respondents to rate satisfaction with communications between management and employees in their organization in a separate part of the survey. However, since this question was only ever fielded in 1992, 2006 and 2012, it is not analyzed here.

[2] While job satisfaction is strictly speaking an ordinal variable – that is, we cannot treat it as an interval variable – research on life satisfaction has shown that under certain reasonable assumptions, it is permissible (Chen et al, 2019). Whatever assumptions one is willing to make, all analysis has been qualitatively replicated using ordinal logit models which explicitly model the ordinal nature of these kinds of scales (available on request).

[3] Survey year, gender, age, whether non-white ethnic group, whether have children, 11 UK regions, holding a degree-level qualification, whether part-time or full-time, whether self-employed or an employee, whether on a temporary or permanent contract, whether their workplace is unionized, three workplace size dummies, four industrial sector indicators, and 205 detailed occupational dummies.

[4] As mentioned in Chapter One, SES unfortunately does not contain information on promotion prospects in the 2017 wave (although it does contain the information in earlier waves) so we do not include it as a constituent component of the GWI. Of course, we would like to have an indicator of this – especially since it appears to be fairly important to workers. But limiting our analysis to just earlier years when it was measured has a number of disadvantages, not least the reduction in sample size.

[5] Economists often refer to this as 'revealed preferences': we can learn more from what people actually do as opposed to what they say they would like to do or are going to do.

[6] Survey year, gender, age, whether non-white ethnic group, whether have children, 11 UK regions, holding a degree-level qualification, whether part-time or full-time, whether self-employed or an employee, whether on a temporary or permanent contract, whether their workplace

is unionized, three workplace size dummies, four industrial sector indicators, and 205 detailed occupational dummies.

[7] What is also surprising is that pay with no further background controls is *negatively* associated with job satisfaction. Further analysis reveals that it is skill-use opportunities that 'flips' the sign. So, in general, job satisfaction is higher in higher-paying jobs: it is positively correlated. But skill-use opportunities are also greater in higher-paying jobs. Pay is only negatively correlated with job satisfaction for a given level of skill-use opportunity.

[8] See, for instance, Zhou, Zou et al (2017) for a study on the UK labour market concerning this phenomenon, including how it interacts with occupational change.

[9] See Clark and Georgellis (2013) for a study looking at well-being adaptation to variety of life events in the UK.

[10] See the now classic study by Clark and Oswald (1996) on this in the UK.

[11] Georgellis et al (2019).

[12] See Steel et al (2019) for a meta-analysis on this point.

[13] See for instance, Williams and Gardiner (2018) for a UK study exploring how different aspects of personality relate to pay and job satisfaction.

[14] The same might not be said if an aspect of job quality decreased.

Chapter Three

[1] Indeed, this is the most common way it is done in policy and research that attempts to combine multiple dimensions of job quality into a single index. See Muñoz de Bustillo et al (2011) for a comprehensive review.

[2] Carnegie (2018).

[3] The SES does include information on satisfaction with relations with colleagues, supervisors and managers but these are also outcomes of job quality rather than the quality of the job itself.

[4] In the 2017 wave of the SES, hours insecurity measures were added (see Felstead et al [2020] for a thorough analysis of them and the issue more generally). However, given we are interested in occupations, the sample sizes of the single 2017 wave are too small for an occupational analysis on its own. We leave the topic of how hours insecurity is stratified across the occupational structure to further research once more data is collected. In the meantime, Koumenta and Williams (2019) provide an occupational analysis of zero-hours contracts (a type of contract associated with hours insecurity).

[5] Dickerson and Green (2012).

[6] For instance, see Koumenta and Williams (2019) for an academic treatment of the theory and evidence on the zero-hours contracts. They

find that zero-hours contracts make up less than 3 per cent of the labour market. Another more recent area of concern are platform workers. Again, these make up a small fraction of the labour market. In this sense, this book is really about the quality of work for the 'many', the other 97 per cent of workers not engaged in these quite niche, though probably often very low quality, forms of employment.

[7] These are recodes of SOC2000 4-digit occupations – recoded to ensure samples sizes of >10 in each occupation cell in the pooled 2006, 2012 and 2017 SES waves.

[8] Running the analysis on different survey years separately and also excluding occupation dummies results in almost identical coefficients.

[9] For a comparative example, see Clark (2005). Such an approach was also taken in sociological studies looking at the job desirability hierarchy in the UK (Mills, 2007) and the US (Jencks et al, 1988).

[10] This is an attractive feature of the GWI. It shares a feature with the pioneering work on welfare function by Anthony Atkinson. Atkinson – perhaps the most influential researcher on inequality of his generation – surmised that summary measures of inequality (such as the Gini coefficient) are inadequate by themselves as they do not take into consideration societal preferences for levels of inequality, and so developed a measure that does.

[11] Clark (2003).

[12] For instance, workers may self-select into occupations based on some unobserved factors.

[13] Note the life satisfaction estimates come from just the 2017 SES sample given it was only measured in that wave and not the others.

Chapter Four

[1] For instance, see Weeden and Grusky (2012) wherein detailed occupations are connected to 39 measures of life chances, attitudes and behaviours on nationally representative samples in the United States. They also find the connections have generally been strengthening and not weakening over time.

[2] Interested readers are referred to Wright (2005) which outlines the main perspectives and debates.

[3] See Rose and Pevalin (2003) and Rose and Pevalin (2005).

[4] It is called the European Socio-Economic Classification (E-SEC). See Rose and Harrison (2006) for more details.

[5] This conjecture has been validated in many ways and over time, see Williams (2017a) for an up-to-date UK assessment. It has also been validated in other contexts. For instance, see Zou (2015) for its applicability to China.

[6] For managerial occupations, it is further divided based on the size of the workplace. The ONS provides an excellent and brief overview of NS-SEC on their website: https://www.ons.gov.uk/methodology/classificationsandstandards/otherclassifications/thenationalstatisticssocioeconomicclassificationnssecrebasedonsoc2010

[7] For more details, see https://www.ons.gov.uk/methodology/classificationsandstandards/standardoccupationalclassificationso

[8] For more details on the International Standard Classification of Occupations, see https://www.ilo.org/public/english/bureau/stat/isco

[9] See Williams (2017a).

[10] They are also decomposable for specific respondents, not just groups.

[11] For instance, the 90–10, the 90–50 and 50–10 ratios, as well as the coefficient of variation.

[12] For UK evidence on this point, see Williams (2013, 2017b).

[13] Because the NS-SEC schema classifies occupations according to whether self-employed and whether an employee has supervision duties (and workplace size if in managerial occupations), occupations may belong to more than one NS-SEC category – hence we report modal classes here. In practice, the vast majority of respondents in a given occupation belong to the same NS-SEC category (median = 95 per cent).

[14] Most of these occupations also require a licence and therefore involve rule-based working practices. Other research has shown that licensed occupations tend to have lower intrinsic job quality relative to other similarly skilled occupations (Williams and Koumenta, 2020).

[15] McGovern et al (2007: 268).

Chapter Five

[1] Frey and Osborne (2013).

[2] ONS (2019b).

[3] For instance, Goos et al (2009, 2014).

[4] Goos and Manning (2007).

[5] Wright and Dwyer (2003).

[6] DBIS (2013).

[7] More recent empirical research has shown that the rich have got richer, but so have the poorer, just by not as much. In the decade since the financial crisis of 2008/09, wage growth has stagnated (except for the very top) and overall wage inequality has remained stable. Trends are different across countries, of course.

[8] Oesch and Piccitto (2019) explore sensitivities in changes in the occupational structure in Germany, Spain, Sweden and the United Kingdom according to different ways of ranking occupations. While not strictly looking at job quality, they explored redefining the occupational hierarchy

in four ways plausibly correlated with occupational fulfilment potential (pay, educational requirements, occupational prestige and job satisfaction). They found a general upgrading the occupational structure since the early 1990s across all these measures and countries. They argue their evidence counters what they term the 'polarization myth'.

[9] Available from the authors on request. We report the analyses done this way as it is likely to be the most reliable way to do it, in that pooling adjacent years reduces random year-to-year variability and using higher levels of aggregation of the occupational classification is too coarse, given the considerable heterogeneity in growth rates within three-digit occupations.

[10] See Oesch and Rodríguez Menés (2010) who examine four European countries, including the UK, and find the growth in jobs in low-paying occupations was only observed in countries where there was a large influx of Eastern European immigrants. A similar pattern for the US is found with respect to Hispanic immigrants (Wright and Dwyer, 2003).

[11] To keep this analysis consistent with the other analyses in this chapter addressing the polarization thesis, we define NS-SEC category based solely on the respondent's occupation and not the supplementary information on employment status, managerial and supervision status, and workplace size. This is why there are only six classes here: small employers and own-account workers are merged into other classes with employees.

[12] See ONS (2019b). One reason why we used the ONS' automation potential scores over others is that they are coded to the same occupational classification schema (SOC 2000) used in the SES. Another reason is that they were developed specifically for the UK context.

[13] Incidentally, in other analysis (not shown but available from the authors), occupations with the highest automation potential are the occupations that declined the most 1980s to present, whereas those occupations with the lowest automation potential are those that have grown the most.

[14] For instance, see Gallie et al (2004).

[15] Most notably Karasek and Theorell (1990), whose job demands-control model has been very influential and well-supported empirically.

Chapter Six

[1] While latest policy has not settled on an index being used as a national measure, the possibility has not been ruled out (Carnegie, 2018). We

believe there is great need for one to be used to complement the dashboard approach, along the lines of the GWI.

[2] Carnegie (2018).

[3] Koumenta and Williams (2019).

[4] Zhou, Wu et al (2017).

[5] Zhou, Zou et al (2017).

References

Atkinson, A.B. (1970) On the Measurement of Inequality. *Journal of Economic Theory*. 2(3): 244–263.

Bell, D. (1974) *The Coming of Post-industrial Society: A Venture in Social Forecasting*. London: Heinemann Educational.

Blauner, R. (1964) *Alienation and Freedom: The Factory Worker and his Industry*. Chicago: University of Chicago Press.

Braverman, H. (1974) *Labor and Monopoly Capital: The Degradation of Work in the Twentieth Century*. New York: Monthly Review Press.

Burchell, B., Sehnbruch, K., Piasna, A. and Agloni, A. (2014) The Quality of Employment and Decent Work: Definitions, Methodologies, and Ongoing Debates. *Cambridge Journal of Economics*. 38(2): 459–477.

Carnegie (2018) *Measuring Good Work: The Final Report of the Measuring Job Quality Working Group*. Dunfermline: Carnegie Trust UK. Available at: https://d1ssu070pg2v9i.cloudfront.net/pex/carnegie_uk_trust/2018/09/03132405/Measuring-Good-Work-FINAL-03-09-18.pdf

Carnegie (2020) *Can Good Work Solve the Productivity Puzzle?* Dunfermline: Carnegie Trust UK. Available at: https://d1ssu070pg2v9i.cloudfront.net/pex/carnegie_uk_trust/2020/01/13104243/Can-good-work-solve-the-productivity-puzzle-FINAL.pdf

Cazes, S., Hijzen, A. and Saint-Martin, A. (2015) *Measuring and Assessing Job Quality: The OECD Job Quality Framework*. OECD Social, Employment and Migration Working Paper, No. 174. Paris: OECD Publishing.

Chen, L.-Y., Oparina, E., Powdthavee, N. and Srisuma, S. (2019) Have Econometric Analyses of Happiness Data Been Futile? A Simple Truth about Happiness Scales. IZA DP No. 12152. Bonn: IZA (Institute of Labor Economics). Available at: http://ftp.iza.org/dp12152.pdf

CIPD (Chartered Institute of Personnel and Development) (2017) *Understanding and Measuring Job Quality: Part 1 – Thematic Literature Review*. London: CIPD. Available at: https://www.cipd.co.uk/Images/understanding-and-measuring-job-quality-1_tcm18-33193.pdf

CIPD (2018) *Understanding and Measuring Job Quality: Part 2 – Indicators of Job Quality*. London: CIPD. Available at: https://www.cipd.co.uk/Images/understanding-and-measuring-job-quality-2_tcm18-36524.pdf

CIPD (2019) *UK Working Lives: The CIPD Job Quality Index*. London: CIPD. Available at: https://www.cipd.co.uk/Images/uk-working-lives-2019-v1_tcm18-58585.pdf

Clark, A. (2003) Looking for Labour Market Rents with Subjective Data. Unpublished mimeo. Available at: http://www.parisschoolofeconomics.com/clark-andrew/iiwjs6.pdf

Clark, A. (2005) What Makes a Good Job? Evidence from OECD Countries. In S. Bazen, C. Lucifora and W. Salverda (eds) *Job Quality and Employer Behaviour*. London: Palgrave Macmillan, pp 11–30.

Clark, A. and Georgellis, Y. (2013) Back to Baseline in Britain: Adaptation in the British Household Panel Survey. *Economica*. 80(319): 496–512.

Clark, A. and Oswald, A. (1996) Satisfaction and Comparison Income. *Journal of Public Economics*. 61(3): 359–381.

DBEIS (Department for Business, Energy and Industrial Strategy) (2017) *Good Work: The Taylor Review of Modern Working Practices*. London: DBEIS. Available at: https://assets.publishing.service.gov.uk/government/uploads/system/uploads/attachment_data/file/627671/good-work-taylor-review-modern-working-practices-rg.pdf

DBIS (Department for Business, Innovation and Skills) (2013) *Hollowing Out and the Future of the Labour Market*. BIS Research Paper No. 134. London: DBIS. Available at: https://assets.publishing.service.gov.uk/government/uploads/system/uploads/attachment_data/file/250206/bis-13-1213-hollowing-out-and-future-of-the-labour-market.pdf

Dickerson, A. and Green, F. (2012) Fears and Realisations of Employment Insecurity. *Labour Economics*. 19(2): 198–210.

Doeringer, P.B. and Piore, M.J. (1985) *Internal Labor Markets and Manpower Analysis*. New York: M.E. Sharpe.

Edwards, R. (1979) *Contested Terrain: The Transformation of the Workplace in the Twentieth Century*. New York: Basic Books.

Eurofound (2002) *Quality of Work and Employment in Europe: Issues and Challenges*. Foundation Paper No. 1. Dublin: Eurofound. Available at: https://www.eurofound.europa.eu/publications/foundation-paper/2002/working-conditions/quality-of-work-and-employment-in-europe-issues-and-challenges-foundation-paper-no-1-february-2002

Fair Work Convention (2016) *Fair Work Framework 2016*. Glasgow: Fair Work Convention. Available at: https://www.fairworkconvention.scot/wp-content/uploads/2018/12/Fair-Work-Convention-Framework-PDF-Full-Version.pdf

Felstead, A., Gallie, D. and Green, F. (eds) (2015) *Unequal Britain at Work*. Oxford: Oxford University Press.

Felstead, A., Gallie, D., Green, F. and Henseke, G. (2019) Conceiving, Designing and Trailing a Short-Form Measure of Job Quality: A Proof-of-Concept Study. *Industrial Relations Journal*. 50(1): 2–19.

Felstead, A., Gallie, D., Green, F. and Henseke, G. (2020) Unpredictable Times: The Extent, Characteristics and Correlates of Insecure Hours of Work in Britain. *Industrial Relations Journal*. 51(1/2): 34–57.

Felstead, A., Gallie, D., Inanc, H. and Green, F. (2014) Skills and Employment Surveys Series Dataset, 1986, 1992, 1997, 2001, 2006, and 2012 [computer file] (2nd edn). Colchester, Essex: UK Data Archive [distributor].

Frey, C. and Osborne, M. (2017) The Future of Employment: How Susceptible are Jobs to Computerisation? *Technological Forecasting and Social Change*. 114: 254–280.

Gallie, D. (ed) (2007) *Employment Regimes and the Quality of Work*. Oxford: Oxford University Press.

Gallie, D., Felstead, A. and Green, F. (2004) Changing Patterns of Task Discretion in Britain. *Work, Employment and Society*. 18(2): 243–266.

Georgellis, Y., Garcia, S.M., Gregoriou, A. and Ozbilgin, M. (2019) Pay Referents and Satisfaction with Pay: Does Occupational Proximity Matter? *British Journal of Management*. 30(3): 578–592.

Goldthorpe, J.H. (2007) Social Class and the Differentiation of Employment Contracts. In J.H. Goldthorpe (ed) *On Sociology (Volume Two): Illustration and Retrospect*. Stanford, CA: Stanford University Press.

Goldthorpe, J.H. (2016) *Sociology as a Population Science*. Cambridge: Cambridge University Press.

Goldthorpe, J.H. and McKnight, A. (2006) The Economic Basis of Social Class. In S.L. Morgan, D.B. Grusky and G.S. Fields (eds) *Mobility and Inequality: Frontiers of Research in Sociology and Economics*. Stanford, CA: Stanford University Press, pp 109–136.

Goos, M. and Manning, A. (2007) Lousy and Lovely Jobs: The Rising Polarization of Work in Britain. *The Review of Economics and Statistics*. 89(1): 118–133.

Goos, M., Manning, A. and Salomons, A. (2009) Job Polarization in Europe. *American Economic Review*. 99 (2): 58–63.

Goos, M., Manning, A. and Salomons, A. (2014) Explaining Job Polarization: Routine-Biased Technological Change and Offshoring. *American Economic Review*. 104(8): 2509–2526.

Grimshaw, D., Fagan, C., Hebson, G. and Tavora, I. (eds) (2017) *Making Work More Equal: A New Labour Market Segmentation Approach*. Manchester: Manchester University Press.

Grote, G. and Guest, D. (2017) The Case for Reinvigorating Quality of Working Life Research. *Human Relations*. 70(2): 149–167.

Hackman, J.R. and Oldham, G.R. (1980) *Work Redesign*. Reading, MA: Addison-Wesley.

HM Government (2018) *Good Work: A Response to the Taylor Review of Modern Working Practices*. London: Department for Business, Energy and Industrial Strategy. Available at: https://www.gov.uk/government/publications/government-response-to-the-taylor-review-of-modern-working-practices

IFOW (Institute for the Future of Work) (2019) *The Future of Good Work: The Foundation of a Modern Moral Economy*. London: IFOW. Available at: https://static1.squarespace.com/static/5aa269bbd274cb0df1e696c8/t/5c64296ce4966bbbfb9fe539/1550068077405/Full+paper+-+The%2BFuture%2Bof%2BGood%2BWork-v7-2.11.18.pdf

Jencks, C., Perman, L. and Rainwater, L. (1988) What Is a Good Job? A New Measure of Labor-Market Success. *American Journal of Sociology*. 93(6): 1322–1357.

Kalleberg, A.L. (2011) *Good Jobs, Bad Jobs*. New York: Russell Sage Foundation.

Karasek, R. and Theorell, T. (1990) *Healthy Work: Stress, Productivity, and the Reconstruction of Working Life*. New York: Basic Books.

Koumenta, M. and Williams, M. (2019) An Anatomy of Zero-Hour Contracts in the United Kingdom. *Industrial Relations Journal*. 50(1): 20–40.

Lambert, P.S. and Bihagen, B. (2014) Using Occupation-Based Social Classifications. *Work, Employment, and Society*. 28(3): 481–494.

Mayo, E. (1933) *The Human Problems of an Industrialized Civilization*. New York: MacMillan Co.

McGovern, P., Hills, M., Mills, C. and White, M. (2007) *Market, Class, and Employment*. Oxford: Oxford University Press.

Mills, C. (2007) Unequal Jobs: Job Quality and Job Satisfaction. In P. McGovern, M. Hills, C. Mills and M. White (eds) *Market, Class, and Employment*. Oxford: Oxford University Press, pp 233–282.

Muñoz de Bustillo, R., Fernández-Macías, E., Antón, J.-I. and Esteve, F. (2011) *Measuring More than Money: The Social Economics of Job Quality*. Cheltenham: Edward Elgar.

National Research Council (2010) A Database for a Changing Economy: Review of the Occupational Information Network (O★NET). Washington, DC: The National Academies Press. https://doi.org/10.17226/12814.

Nickell, S. (1982) The Determinants of Occupational Success in Britain. *Review of Economic Studies*. 49(1): 43–53.

Oesch, D. and Piccitto, G. (2019) The Polarization Myth: Occupational Upgrading in Germany, Spain, Sweden, and the UK, 1992–2015. *Work and Occupations*. 46(4): 441–469.

Oesch, D. and Rodríguez Menés, J. (2010) Upgrading or Polarization? Occupational Change in Britain, Germany, Spain and Switzerland, 1990–2008. *Socio-Economic Review*. 9(3): 503–531.

ONS (Office for National Statistics) (2017) New Earnings Survey Panel Dataset, 1975–2016: Secure Access [data collection] (7th edn). London: ONS & UK Data Service. Study number 6706. Available at: https://doc.ukdataservice.ac.uk/doc/6706/mrdoc/UKDA/UKDA_Study_6706_Information.htm

ONS (2019a) Job Quality Indicators in the UK – Hours, Pay and Contracts: 2018. London: ONS. Available at: https://www.ons.gov.uk/employmentandlabourmarket/peopleinwork/employmentandemployeetypes/articles/jobqualityindicatorsintheeukhourspayandcontracts/2018

ONS (2019b) The Probability of Automation in England: 2011 and 2017. London: ONS. Available at: https://www.ons.gov.uk/employmentandlabourmarket/peopleinwork/employmentandemployeetypes/articles/theprobabilityofautomationinengland/2011and2017/pdf

Piketty, T. (2014) *Capital in the Twenty-First Century*. London: The Belknap Press of Harvard University Press.

Reich, R. (1991) *The Work of Nations: Preparing Ourselves for 21st Century Capitalism*. London: Simon & Schuster.

Rizter, G. (1993) *McDonaldization of Society*. Thousand Oaks: Pine Forge Press.

Rose D. and Harrison, E. (2010) *Social Class in Europe: An Introduction to the European Socio-economic Classification*. London: Routledge.

Rose, D. and Pevalin, D.J. (2003) *A Researcher's Guide to the National Statistics Socio-economic Classification*. London: Sage.

Rose, D. and Pevalin, D.J. (2005) *The National Statistics Socio-Economic Classification: Origins, Development and Use*. Basingstoke: Palgrave Macmillan.

Steel, P., Schmidt, J., Bosco, F. and Uggerslev, K. (2019) The Effects of Personality on Job Satisfaction and Life Satisfaction: A Meta-analytic Investigation Accounting for Bandwidth–Fidelity and Commensurability. *Human Relations*. 72(2): 217–247.

Warr, P. (1987) *Work, Unemployment, and Mental Health*. Oxford: Oxford University Press.

Weeden, K. and Grusky, D. (2012) The Three Worlds of Inequality. *American Journal of Sociology*. 117(6): 1723–1785.

Welsh Government (2019) *Fair Work Wales: Report of the Fair Work Commission*. Cardiff: Welsh Government. Available at: https://gov.wales/sites/default/files/publications/2019-05/fair-work-wales.pdf

Williams, M. (2013) Occupations and British Wage Inequality, 1970s–2000s. *European Sociological Review*. 29(4): 841–857.

Williams, M. (2017a) Occupational Stratification in Contemporary Britain: Occupational Class and the Wage Structure in the Wake of the Great Recession, *Sociology*. 51(6): 1299–1317.

Williams, M. (2017b) An Old Model of Social Class? Job Characteristics and the NS-SEC Schema. *Work, Employment and Society*. 31(1): 153–165.

Williams, M. and Gardiner, E. (2018) The Power of Personality at Work: Core Self-Evaluations and Earnings in the United Kingdom. *Human Resource Management Journal*. 28(1): 45–60.

Williams, M., Zhou, Y. and Zou, M. (2019) The Rise in Pay for Performance Among Higher Managerial and Professional Occupations in Britain. *Work, Employment and Society*. https://journals.sagepub.com/doi/10.1177/0950017019841552.

Williams, M. and Koumenta, M. (2020) Occupational Closure and Job Quality: The Case of Occupational Licensing in Britain. *Human Relations*. 73(5): 711–736.

Wright, E.O. (ed) (2005) *Approaches to Class Analysis*. Cambridge: Cambridge University Press.

Wright, E.O. and Dwyer, R. (2003) The Patterns of Job Expansions in the USA: A Comparison of the 1960s and 1990s. *Socio-Economic Review*. 1(3): 289–325.

Zhou, Y., Wu, C.H., Zou, M. and Williams, M. (2017) A Longitudinal Study of the Impact of Occupational Mobility on Job Satisfaction Trajectory: Individual Differences in Neuroticism. *Academy of Management Best Paper Proceedings*. Briarcliff Manor, NY: Academy of Management.

Zhou, Y., Zou, M., Williams, M. and Tabvuma, V. (2017) Is the Grass Greener on the Other Side? A Longitudinal Study of the Impact of Occupation Change on Employee Job Satisfaction. *Journal of Vocational Behavior*. 99: 66–78.

Zhou, Y., Zou, M., Woods, S. and Wu, C.H. (2019) The Restorative Effect of Work After Unemployment: An Intraindividual Analysis of Subjective Well-Being Recovery Through Reemployment. *Journal of Applied Psychology*. 104(9): 1195–1206.

Zou, M. (2015) Employment Relations and Social Stratification in Contemporary Urban China: Does Goldthorpe's Class Theory Still Work? *Sociology*. 49: 1133–1150.

Index